OLE BILL
LONDON BUSES AND THE FIRST WORLD WAR

by Dr William D Ward
Edited by David Lawrence

Published in 2014

London Transport Museum
Covent Garden Piazza
London WC2E 7BB
Tel +44 (0)20 7379 6344

Design by LTM Design

ISBN 978-1-871829-22-8

Dedication
This book is respectfully dedicated to the 9,548 members of the London General Omnibus Company staff who served with the armed forces in the First World War of 1914–18. In particular we remember the 1,170 who were only issued with one-way tickets.

Picture credits
The majority of images reproduced in this book are from the London Transport Museum collection. We are grateful to the following individuals and institutions for providing additional material:

Terry Gosling collection (p.83)
William Ward collection (p.7, p.79)
Michael Young collection (p.44, p.53, p.77 p.101)
The Tank Museum (p.83)

Cover image
Buses at Grove Park, 1914.
Michael Young collection

CONTENTS

FOREWORD 02

PREFACE 03

ACKNOWLEDGEMENTS 05

CHAPTER ONE: Early pioneers: experimental troop transport by bus, 1908–09 07

CHAPTER TWO: The London B-type bus: design, manufacture and service, 1910–14 19

CHAPTER THREE: Single deck bus ambulances of the Royal Navy, 1914–18 23

CHAPTER FOUR: Daimler buses of the Royal Navy, 1914–15 27

CHAPTER FIVE: Military B-type buses, 1914–19 41

CHAPTER SIX: The Auxiliary (Omnibus) Park MT, 1917–19 55

CHAPTER SEVEN: Buses converted for other war uses 65

CHAPTER EIGHT: Armoured B-types, Artillery B-types, B-type and Daimler military lorries . . . 77

CHAPTER NINE: Buses and their Home Front war service, 1914–21 87

CHAPTER TEN: *Aprés la guerre fini*: war buses in peacetime 95

APPENDIX 1:   Military colour schemes and markings of war buses 101

APPENDIX 2:   Preserved buses 106

GLOSSARY OF SPECIALIST TERMS 108

FURTHER READING 109

INDEX 110

FOREWORD

Dr William Ward contacted the Museum late in 2013 after hearing about our 'Battlebus' restoration project. Bill had done extensive research on the B-type bus at war over many years and had a finished, but as yet unpublished, manuscript. He was pleasantly surprised to find that we too were interested in his passion.

The London bus drivers' contribution to the war effort of 1914-1918 is a little known aspect of the First World War, which London Transport Museum used to create the narrative of civilian wartime London for our exhibition 'Goodbye Piccadilly'. Placing the buses and their crews in the transformation of London as the key centre for wartime operations, has given a fresh and civilian perspective on the Capital's first experience of total war. The story embraces the women who joined the transport workforce for the first time as cleaners, conductors and station staff, and also those Londoners who suffered aerial attack at home for the first time in history.

The extreme experiences of the Western Front - trench warfare, artillery bombardment, mud, barbed wire and the presence of death - were made all the more poignant by their proximity to home. London was only a day's travel away and the guns could even be heard in the Capital. In these extraordinary conditions, men looked for symbols of the normal lives they had left behind - the letter from home, the newspaper - and deployed black humour to mitigate the horror, smiling at Bruce Bairnsfather's 'Ole Bill cartoons, naming a trench 'Bond Street' or giving new lyrics to familiar songs. Just behind the fighting lines, the Tommies found columns of buses, those most ordinary symbols of everyday London, which like them were wrenched from the Capital's streets to ply their trade in the maelstrom of war.

We are delighted to have worked with Bill to publish this book, securing such a strong historical base for our restoration of a B-type bus to wartime condition and our loan of Ole Bill himself from the Imperial War Museum for the 'Goodbye Piccadilly' exhibition. Bill Ward has been a joy to work with and his book brings to life the busmen's story. This book Ole Bill will accompany 'Battlebus', the restored B2737, to Year of the Bus events: to the Western Front from the autumn of 2014, and to the Remembrance Parade in November 2014, thus commemorating the London drivers who volunteered in the service of their country to take themselves and their buses far beyond their normal 'end of route'.

Sam Mullins, Director
London Transport Museum

Opposite
Ole Bill in the Armistice Day parade, c1920.
1998/75682

PREFACE

In November every year, on Remembrance Sunday, representatives of the whole nation parade past the Cenotaph in Whitehall, London. The last section to pass is always a group of London transport staff. For decades they marched in the company of a very special vehicle: a bright red open-topped double-decker London bus. This was B-type bus number B43, built in 1911 by the London General Omnibus Company (LGOC) at its factory in Walthamstow, north east London. B43 served on the London streets operating from Old Ford Garage on routes 8 and 25 until it was hurriedly requisitioned by the War Office on 18 September 1914 and sent to France.[1] It served throughout the war and in 1919 was repurchased by the LGOC who, after a rapid overhaul, put B43 back into service as a 'Traffic Emergency Bus'. Following a further overhaul it continued to serve from Dalston garage on routes 8 and 9.

After the war, King George V had expressed a desire to see some of the bus drivers who had served in France, and one of their buses. On 14 February 1920 Driver James Melton steered B43, with twenty-five wartime colleagues aboard, through the gates of Buckingham Palace where they were inspected by the King. The monarch remarked that it was the first time he had ever boarded a London bus. To mark this occasion the bus was specially decorated. A brass shell was mounted on the dashboard in front of the driving position, and ornate 'B43' plates were made for the bonnet sides. One further adornment made at this time would secure for B43 the name by which it is commonly known: Ole Bill. Bruce Bairnsfather created a First World War cartoon character called 'Old Bill'.[2] Such was the character's popularity as a representation of the millions of ordinary people who went to war, many souvenirs were made in his likeness. A brass bust of 'Old Bill' was fitted to B43 as a radiator cap when it went to be received by the King. The title, derived from

Bairnsfather's famous cartoon 'If you know a better 'ole...', was later given to the memorial bus. Ole Bill carries the names of battles such as Antwerp and Ypres where the buses served and the titles of famous regiments and their badges, to commemorate the service given by London buses during the First World War of 1914-18.

In 1920 after receiving a complete new body and mechanical repair, B43 was handed over to the Auxiliary Omnibus Companies Association (AOCA), a group of veteran Army bus drivers. The AOCA used it to attend Armistice Day parades and the funerals of their members. B43 also helped raise money for the Royal British Legion Poppy Appeal. On 30 April 1970, after nearly 60 years of service Ole Bill was presented to the Imperial War Museum, London to represent the buses that went to France in 1914 to provide the hard-pressed British Army with much needed motor transport. During 2014, Ole Bill formed part of the Goodbye Piccadilly exhibition at the London Transport Museum, Covent Garden, London. At other times, this colourful icon can be seen, looking a little incongruous perhaps amongst the khaki and field grey weapons of destruction, in the collection of the Imperial War Museum. Written using detailed study of the first-hand accounts preserved in official War Diaries, and extensive research, this is the story of B43 Ole Bill, and the other London buses that went to war.

Dr William D Ward, Colchester, England 2014

NB. An earlier version of chapter 4 was first published in French in the January 1994 edition of Tank Museum News, the journal of the Belgian Musée Royal de l'Armée in Brussels, under the title 'Des Autobus à Imperiale Londiniens à Anvers'.

ACKNOWLEDGEMENTS

I have tried to give proper credit to any sources I have used, wherever the copyright has expired, and to seek permission wherever I have been able to find the copyright holder. If I have used any source incorrectly I will happily acknowledge it.

There are few works on this subject and much of it has had to be assembled from fragments of information. As an example, the story of the 1st Battalion of the London Scottish at the First Battle of Ypres and their bus transport was assembled from a study of the following texts: *Flanders Then and Now; TOT Magazine; The London Scottish in the Great War* by Lieutenant-Colonel J H Lindsay; Captain F C Hitchcock's *Stand-To – A Diary of the Trenches; Battleground Europe* by Nigel Cave; War Diaries of the 1st Auxiliary Omnibus Coy and the Royal Marine Transport at the National Archives, Kew, Surrey; visits to the London Scottish Regimental Museum, London Transport Museum, Documentatiecentrum (formerly Documentatiecentrum Dr A. Caenepeel), In Flanders Fields Museum, Ypres, Belgium, and to Bus House Cemetery, Ypres, Belgium. Much of the other detail in the book has been like doing a lot of simultaneous jigsaw puzzles with most of the pieces missing and no idea of what the final picture should be. I have had to read the whole of a regimental history to find a line or two of an occasion when they travelled by bus, or even had bus transport promised, which failed to arrive. Sometimes the buses turn out to be French - Parisian - buses in military service - but that is another story.

I would like to thank the following individuals for their valuable help: Patricia Austin, former Librarian, London Transport Museum; Peter Bailey and the late John Baumann of the Miniature Armoured Fighting Vehicles Association; Ed Bartholomew, former Photographic Librarian, Royal Marines Museum, Eastney, Hampshire;

the late J M Cummings, London Historical Research Group, Omnibus Society; G W Dodson, Marketing Manager, Eastern National Ltd, Chelmsford; David Fletcher, former Librarian, Archive & Reference Library, the Tank Museum, Bovington, Dorset; John Haynes, former Honorary Curator, London Scottish Regimental Museum; the Trustees of the London Scottish Regiment; Staff at the Imperial War Museum Photo library, London. Georges Mazy, Curator, Tank Museum, Musée Royal de l'Armée, Brussels; Dr Jack de Moor, Antwerp; The cheerful and helpful staff at The National Archives, Kew; R D O'Kill; the late G J Robbins; A E Woodbridge, formerly of the Household Cavalry Museum, Windsor; Lieutenant Colonel Michael Young, formerly of Royal Logistic Corps Journal, Camberley, Surrey.

I would especially like to thank my family: my son Dr William A Ward - for his many searches in the Transport section of Leicester University Library and on the Internet; my daughter Fiona Dyas - who found a bus number plate in Ypres; my wife Marilyn who has travelled to some very odd corners of the world with me and put up with a great deal at home also, and my son Ian. Ian is now a teacher of French in Australia and used to think we kept going to France to improve his French, when in fact we were doing bus research too.

I would also like to thank the staff at London Transport Museum who made it possible for this work to be published. In particular Sam Mullins, Director and Dr David Lawrence, Research Fellow for his sensitive editorial work in preparing my manuscript; Simon Murphy, Curator for his work on picture research and image captions; Caroline Warhurst, Librarian for managing the copy-editing process; and Sau-Fun Mo, Head of Design, for a strong design supporting this unique story.

Opposite
Ole Bill at the London Transport Museum, 2014.
Martin Tulloch

What is this that roareth thus?
Can it be a Motor Bus?
Yes, the smell and hideous hum
Indicat Motorem Bum.

The Motor Bus, by A D Godley (1856–1925)

The idea of using motor buses to transport troops did not suddenly occur to the British Government War Office at the outbreak of the conflict in August 1914. Their use had been tried out on a number of occasions well before that date. The earliest recorded British bus operator to utilize his vehicles to carry soldiers was Thomas Clarkson of Chelmsford. He had problems in selling the steam buses he manufactured, and hoped that he could sell some of them to the government, by demonstrating their effectiveness and value for troop transport. In 1908 Clarkson persuaded Captain W G Wenley, one of the officers of the Essex Territorials who was involved in a war games exercise, to issue a challenge that he could get an advance guard from Chelmsford to the River Crouch in 90 minutes. (His grandson says that quite serious money was involved in a bet.) None of his seniors, who were only used to the speed of marching troops and their horse-drawn transport, believed this was possible and so a demonstration was arranged. The soldiers of the 5th Battalion, Essex Regiment (Territorial Force), who were to take part in the exercise, were told it would take place on a Sunday, but not the exact date. Some were so keen that they were reported to have slept in their uniforms for several Saturday nights so as to be ready more quickly. Finally, on Sunday 6 December 1908 the exercise took place. It was reported very fully in the *Essex Chronicle*:

'A surprise alarm of invasion was sounded on the fire hooter at Chelmsford at 9.15am. In ten minutes the Territorials were assembling at the Drill Hall and in a quarter of an hour the supply column was on the move. In three quarters of an hour, or to be exact 10.02am a hundred and twenty-eight men with officers and Special Correspondents were off in the steam cars and at nine minutes past eleven the whole disembarked in one minute at Latchingdon, fourteen miles away, with full equipment. Captain Wenley, the leader, thus proved his point with twenty-one minutes in hand. And under the most adverse

weather conditions because it rained pitilessly the whole time and the roads and lanes were in a state of mud resembling treacle. En route, too, there was a long and steep hill at Danbury, up which the motor buses climbed gaily, notwithstanding the rise here is some 300 feet from Chelmsford…The buses are beautifully upholstered and lit by electricity generated as they travel, and as we remarked at the time, riding in them on such an occasion was like riding to war in a first class carriage. Our representative travelled in one of the four omnibuses, each carrying forty-one passengers, and a fifth bus carried fifty. There was a steam car and a steam van. All the vehicles were manufactured by Mr Clarkson at Chelmsford and the inventor himself accompanied the expedition…'.[3]

This exercise was reported to the newly formed Mechanical Transport Committee of the War Office. Captain R K Bignall-Wild, secretary of the committee, suggested a more extensive manoeuvre using hired buses. The public at this time was being bombarded with stories of invasion scares, both in newspapers and books. The scenario of the exercise was that an enemy force had landed in the Thames Estuary and that spies had sabotaged the railway lines to prevent the transport of soldiers. On 18 December 1908 Captain Bignall-Wild asked the London General Omnibus Company (LGOC) if they could provide hired buses to carry a battalion of troops to Shoeburyness. The LGOC had just completed the great amalgamation of London bus companies and each of the three companies involved in the merger provided eight buses, eight De Dion buses from the LGOC, eight Milnes-Daimlers from Vanguard and eight Straker-Squires from the London Road Car Company. There were also three service lorries, one of each make. The army provided a number of staff cars and motorcycles. The whole column was under the control of Frank Searle, chief engineer of the LGOC who led it in his own car.

Opposite
LGOC De Dion-Bouton buses on military exercises in Essex, December 1908.
William Ward collection

At 5.30am on 21 December 1908, a cold and misty morning, the buses left Upton Park garage in London and drove in three columns to Warley Barracks near Brentwood. For the London bus drivers this was an exciting holiday outing and feeling that they were safe in the fog from their chief's observation they started racing each other and the columns became rather muddled. Only a few months before they had been racing each other in earnest through the London streets as they fought for fares, and the rivalry remained. Frank Searle, who we will learn more about below, had a few harsh words to say when the column reached Brentwood. At Warley barracks they embussed (loaded) 500 men, four companies of the 1st Battalion the Norfolk Regiment and one company of the 7th (Territorial) Battalion the Essex Regiment, under the command of Lieutenant Colonel Massey of the Norfolks. Each vehicle carried 26 men plus their packs and equipment.

The buses were then divided up into two columns, which were to travel by different routes. Motorcycle scouts led the columns, which were followed by two buses designated as ambulances and one as a staff bus for officers. There was one Maxim machine gun for each eight buses. The London bus drivers had to learn that these country roads were not up to city standards: they were a cloud of dust in the summer and a sea of mud in the winter. [4] The drivers soon learned to drive on the crown of the road and not near the edge. The first casualty was one of the ambulance buses, which became ditched. One of the buses in this column broke through the road surface up to its axles and needed both lorries to pull it out. At Hadleigh near Southend, the 'enemy' were sighted and the troops debussed to attack them. *Commercial Motor* commented at length on the results of the exercise:

'The distances to be kept and the speeds to be observed will have to be much more carefully ordered. The speed of the column must be that of the slowest machine, and the breakdown lorry must shepherd the lot. Types must be concentrated as much as possible, and "stations" must be kept en route, as in the navy, at settled distances, which should be sufficient to avoid the necessity for wholesale "changing down" when one vehicle in front temporarily slows down slightly. A spare vehicle should be run to every eight or ten, so that mishaps of any kind can be relegated to the care of the breakdown wagon.' [5]

The reporter also suggested that food should be carried for the drivers, as no one had thought to tell them to bring any and no arrangements had been made.

In 1909 the Metropolitan Police Licensing Authority in London introduced new regulations limiting the weight of London buses to 3.5 tons. This revised weight limit meant Thomas Clarkson had to amend his steam bus design, and as he was finding few buyers he decided to set up his own company to operate the vehicles himself. As part of the publicity campaign to advertise the flotation of his new company, Clarkson used his connections with the Territorials to bring his buses to public notice. On 28 May 1909 he carried the soldiers and baggage of the Essex Yeomanry from Chelmsford to their annual camp at Sudbury in Suffolk, using four of his steam buses. In four days the troops covered 150 miles, the steam buses reinforced by a lorry mounting a machine gun, 'an innovation which materially assisted in the signal defeat of the Suffolk Yeomanry'. [6] 'A' and 'C' Squadrons of the Essex Yeomanry, rushed up in the motor buses, crossed the River Blyth by the weakly defended bridge at Blythburgh and turned the enemy right wing, catching the Suffolk Yeomanry in such a scattered state that they could not concentrate by the time the exercise was over. The buses took the men's baggage

Left
Clarkson Steam
Bus in Chelmsford,
one of five carrying
Territorial army
troops on an invasion
exercise in the
Thames Estuary,
June 1909.
1998/71499

home after the exercise to reduce the load on the horses of the transport column.

On 22 June 1909 Clarkson arranged a test run of one of his steam buses from Chelmsford to Folkestone and back in one day. The route involved crossing the Thames by the Woolwich ferry. This run was conducted 'under the observation of a representative of the Director of Transport and Remounts and other gentlemen interested in rapid transport'. The distance of 186 miles was covered in a running time of 13 hours 38 minutes at an average speed of 13.6 miles per hour, 'running punctually to schedule'.[7] A further invasion exercise with the Essex Territorials took place in July 1909 when 160 Territorials were transported from Chelmsford to Colchester. On this occasion five buses were employed, painted white with the fleet name NATIONAL, and bearing on the front of the upper deck the patriotic slogan 'Be Prepared!' and on the side the legends 'Wake Up England!' 'Be Prepared!'. The publicity campaign ended with a great procession of Clarkson steam buses through the streets of London on 30 October 1909 carrying a large party of Chelmsford and Essex notables and a party of Boy Scouts who sent semaphore messages to any military establishment they passed. All this publicity enabled Clarkson to launch his new bus company, which he had christened National to emphasize that he felt his pioneer troop transport had been of national importance.

Clarkson steam buses continued to serve until 1918. They became more valuable during the war when petrol was rationed although the company, ironically, complained of interruptions to the service by demands for buses for troop movements. At the 1914 Annual General Meeting of the National company it was reported that 30 buses had been requisitioned for troop transport by the military authorities in London. In 1919, with the return to normal conditions, the steam buses were no longer able to compete financially with petrol buses and Thomas Clarkson sold out his interest in National. The company immediately bought petrol-driven buses, but true to its patriotic origins would only employ ex-servicemen. Its successor, the Eastern National Bus Company, has since been rebranded as First Essex, and still has its headquarters in Chelmsford.

On 17 March 1909, as a publicity stunt, the infant Automobile Association (AA) offered to transport a battalion of troops from London to Hastings in cars provided by its members. The baggage was carried in hired Napier lorries. The trade journals were not impressed. While giving credit to the AA for their organisation, *Motor Traction* said: 'however, the heavy class of motor vehicle fitted with 'bus or Char-à-banc type of bodies suggests a practical and cheaper solution of the problem'.[8] *Commercial Motor* was more critical still, writing 'which prompt an enquiry as to whether the whole thing could not have been carried out more neatly, and with infinitely less risk…by means of a column, one tenth of the length, composed of motorbuses or char-a-bancs and lorries'.[9] In their history the AA note that they asked if the Army had learned anything useful from the exercise about motor transport. They were told that it had been found that some of the caps of the Irish Guards had been blown off by the wind of the cars' progress and that in future they would be fitted with a chin-strap![10]

The reduction in the weight limits for buses in London by the Metropolitan Police in 1909 also caused problems for the LGOC which had to obtain new buses within the weight restrictions. Initially they gave all their specifications to the Wolseley Company and asked them to design a bus, but this new design had many problems in service. Frank Searle (1874-1948), chief engineer of the LGOC, suggested that it might be better if the company built a bus to its own design at the Walthamstow repair works it had inherited from Vanguard. Frank Searle had been trained as a railway engineer with the Great Western Railway and had taken an interest in buses at an early stage in his career. He had set up his own company to import foreign chassis on which British bus operators could build their own bodies but the venture failed as the buses could not stand up to the demanding working conditions of the London streets. Searle worked for the Arrow bus company for a while and then in February 1907 he joined the LGOC as superintendent of their Mortlake garage in south west London. He was so efficient that within three months he was transferred to the huge chief depot at Cricklewood, where he found 28 different types of motor omnibus in use, together with 300 horses for 30 horse buses.

Searle discovered that only a quarter of the motor buses were in use at any one time. The rest were either broken down or having overhauls. This created a complex problem with storing and selecting the correct spares for vehicle repairs, and the mechanics had little chance to learn the peculiarities of any one model. Searle persuaded the directors of the LGOC to segregate the makes, one to each garage, to simplify the spares problem and to enable the mechanics to concentrate on one type. This was so effective that when the great London bus company amalgamation took place in July 1908, Searle was appointed as chief engineer of the new company. There had been such a serious price war that the three companies involved had been threatened with financial

Left
Cricklewood LGOC
bus garage with De
Dion and Straker-
Squire motor buses,
1908.
1998/75603

Below
Frank Searle in 1921.
1998/40810

ruin. With the rationalisation of services made possible by the combination of the three biggest bus companies in London, a profitable operation became possible. Searle saw the chance to have a standardised model of bus and persuaded the directors to let him build his own design.

The first bus that Searle produced was the X-type in August 1909. Writers at the time rather scathingly called it the Daimler-Wolseley-Straker type because, as Frank Searle himself wrote later, 'In the manufacture of the X-type we cribbed shamelessly, any part of the 28 types which had stood up to the gruelling of the London streets were embodied in it'. The X-type was not received too favourably by the directors of the LGOC, who, at its great unveiling, were all distracted by the return of the bus horses from an army manoeuvre, for which they had been hired out, and had a quite understandable desire to see that the horses were checked for injuries. The

Metropolitan Police Licensing Authority was not too impressed either with the gear-box of the X-type. Gear-boxes of the time were very noisy, said to sound like a machine-gun travelling down the street. Every bus had to have an annual inspection on Wimbledon Common and one anecdote suggests that many motor omnibuses were said to have passed their examinations only by the twin expedients of a gear-box filled with oily sawdust for the day, and a five pound note tucked under the driver's seat.

For his next bus, the B-type, Searle designed a new chain-driven gear-box which was remarkably silent for its day. The B-type proved so reliable that it became the financial salvation of the LGOC, and the company was unwilling to sell vehicles to any other London bus company once they had enough for their own purposes. Even buyers from further afield had to sign undertakings not to allow the buses to be operated in competition with the LGOC.

Above
MET Daimler motor bus, D155, 1913.
1998/89144

Left
B-type chassis at the AEC factory, Walthamstow, 1913.
2013/7925

Some competitors approached the British Daimler Company of Coventry who produced a petro-electric bus of a very innovative new design, the KPL, which was to be used by the Gearless Company. The LGOC immediately bought some patent rights which the new bus was said to infringe, and blocked its production. Daimler then secretly approached Searle and asked him to design a new bus for them.

Searle was unhappy at the LGOC because he felt he had been badly treated by them over the patent rights to his new gear-box (they had abandoned the patent application) and also because he was still employed on a monthly salary with no contract to guarantee job security. The Board of the LGOC somehow got wind of this overture and at a stormy board meeting in May 1911, they insisted that he must immediately sign a contract with them for five years or he would be dismissed. Searle asked for time to consider, and when this was refused, he left to join the Daimler Company. He designed for Daimler a new bus, the CC model. This combined all the good points of the B-type chassis and body with the excellent Silent Knight sleeve-valve engine.

Searle obtained his first order for 100 of the new Daimler buses from the Metropolitan Electric Tramways new company, the Tramways (MET) Omnibus Company, in 1912. The MET had decided to fight the increasing threat to its tram network by operating its own motor bus services. Searle then approached Albert Stanley, chairman of the Underground Electric Railways Company of London (UERL - Underground group), who had also been suffering from the competition of the successful new buses and asked him if he would be interested in buying Daimlers. Stanley offered to buy 250 vehicles, but only if Searle would agree not to sell any to other London bus operators. Searle immediately went back to the MET with this information and got them to increase their order at once to 350 units. Stanley realized that a new price war would damage everyone and arranged a buy-out of both the LGOC and MET by the Underground group. This was the genesis of London Transport. It also meant that when the first Daimler buses entered service in 1913, the MET was worked as a subsidiary of the LGOC: the buses were owned by the MET but run by the LGOC as part of their fleet.

These two vehicles, the B-type and the Daimler CC, both designed by Frank Searle, became the only types of bus considered reliable enough to be used by the British Army in France and Belgium during the First World War. Sergeant Major G Dyas of the Army Service Corps (ASC), perhaps as a former LGOC employee a rather biased witness, wrote in the April 1915 edition of Underground group staff magazine TOT: 'I must speak highly of the durability of the Daimler and 'B' type, as their cars are picked out for the ammunition supply columns, which speaks for itself. Candidly speaking, not only the Government but the whole country, should in future show respect to our 'General' men who have played such a part and revolutionised the old method of transport'. A less biased view was expressed by the writer of the War Diary of the 1st GHQ Ammunition Park, who wrote on 15 January 1916: 'Asked for the replacement of 5 lorries of ancient type to be replaced with B-type, Daimler or Subsidy Leylands. Reply, nothing can be done!'.

Frank Searle also served in France. As Lieutenant Colonel Frank Searle DSO he was chief engineer of the Tank Corps at their Erin workshops near Agincourt, where he was reported as being able to understand the working of everything except the mind of the regular army officer. He took with him to the Tank Workshops several LGOC people including George Rackham, one of the draughtsmen who had assisted him in the design of the B-type bus.

Above
LGOC X-type motor bus No.X35, 1909.
1998/75453

1   Old Ford Garage, Old Ford Road, London E3, was in operation
    1910-17, and 1919-20. Clay Hall Garage was built on the same
    site in 1931, and closed in 1959.

2   (Charles) Bruce Bairnsfather (1887–1959), was a cartoonist
    and writer. He served as a Captain with the 1st Battalion Royal
    Warwickshire Regiment in France during the First World War,
    and began drawing cartoon representations of soldiers in
    1915. Here he conceived the character 'Old Bill', a genial, war-
    weary, regular soldier. Bairnsfather also developed the setting
    of a battlefield shell hole for many of his cartoons, using the
    slang form 'ole in his captions.

3   *Essex Chronicle*, December 1908.

4   The roads in rural Essex were macadamised but not
    tarmacadamised. That is to say, there was a stone dressing on
    the road but it was not sealed.

5   *Commercial Motor*, 24 December 1908.

6   Gerald Rickman, 'The Essex Yeomanry', in *Essex Review*, April
    1957.

7   Archives, Eastern National Ltd., Chelmsford.

8   *Motor Traction*, 20 March 1909.

9   *Commercial Motor*, 25 March 1909.

10 Automobile Association history files.

As I stood upon London Bridge and viewed the mighty throng
Of thousands of people in cabs and 'busses rapidly whirling along,
All furiously driving to and fro,
Up one street and down another as quick as they could go.

Descriptive jottings of London William McGonagall (1825–1902)

THE LONDON B-TYPE BUS:
DESIGN, MANUFACTURE AND SERVICE, 1910–1914

CHAPTER TWO

Opposite
New B-types at
Cricklewood garage,
May 1911.
1998/60205

Left
B-type chassis, 1913.
2013/6826

Frank Searle designed the B-type bus, his most famous work, in 1910. In October 1910, B1, the first of more than 3,486 B-type vehicles, began service on the streets of London. The chassis were built at the Walthamstow works of the London General Omnibus Company, where the works engineer Walter James Iden (1873-1952) developed production lines to mass produce chassis, turning out 30 a week by 1912. Iden's maxim for the B-type was 'High quality of parts and interchangeability'. Enough B-types had been produced by October 1912 for the LGOC's own requirements and the Walthamstow works were separated off as a new company, the Associated Equipment Company (AEC), as it was thought this would make easier to sell the B-type to other bus concerns outside London.

The chassis were built on the flitch plate system. Each component of the chassis frame consisted of an ash plank sandwiched between two steel plates, the whole being bolted and riveted together. This structure gave the best compromise between strength and flexibility. Each chassis was built on a jig to ensure all parts could be used on all buses of the same class. Such carefully engineered flexibility was a major factor in the financial success of the B-type. The wheels had solid tyres; pneumatic tyres were not really advanced enough to be used on heavy vehicles like buses and the large number of horse-shoe nails which littered the streets of London at this date would have made them uneconomical. The front wheels could have either five, six or eight spokes and the rear wheels could have either eight straight pressed steel spokes or eight Y-shaped steel spokes. The engine was a 32hp four-cylinder petrol model, and the gearbox, Searle's own chain-driven design, was mounted far back to even up the weight distribution. The engine was fitted with a 'governor' device to prevent speeds of more than 16mph. This exceeded the Metropolitan Police 12mph speed limit for buses, but during war service abroad, the crews would commonly 'neglect' to maintain the governor and could attain speeds of up to 35mph on good roads, although the average speed for buses in convoy was found to be 10mph, with 12mph as the average speed for a single bus.

The first bodies were built at the Holloway body works of the LGOC, with later examples being constructed elsewhere by subcontractors. Metropolitan Police

Regulations required buses to be 'properly painted', which was interpreted as twelve coats of paint and six coats of varnish. On the top deck, a total of 18 passengers could be accommodated on nine wooden slatted garden bench type double seats. There were five on the left-hand side of the gangway and only four on the right-hand side to allow access from the open rear stairway. The police were adamantly opposed to any sort of upper deck covering in case it imperilled stability, so each seat had a storm apron fitted behind it to give upper deck passengers some protection from the elements in bad weather. The enclosed lower deck featured thinly upholstered lateral benches on each side seating 16, giving a total seating capacity for the vehicle of 34 passengers. Standing passengers were not allowed until the wartime shortage of buses necessitated this concession. Wartime bus shortages also led to the introduction of the requirement for waiting passengers to form an orderly line. This London bye-law made it an offence to jump a bus queue, and the queues were initially controlled by special constables.

Bus destination boards were also strictly regulated by the Police. They had to be of specified dimensions, and even the size of the lettering on them was prescribed. Boards had to be painted in black and white, and any commercial notices on the front or back of the bus had to be in colour, so as not to be confused with the route information. These boards were reversible for the return journey. To take advantage of the commercial opportunity presented by these moving display spaces, every possible surface of the bus was covered with advertisements. Both sides of the exterior carried large panels, and the guard or 'modesty' boards on the stair had adverts inside and out. Advertisements were placed behind each seat and on the ceiling of the lower deck. Even the small ventilation windows had transparent adverts stuck on them. These displays were said to earn enough money to defray the cost of the annual repainting.

Other B-type vehicles

The LGOC also adapted a number of B-type chassis for its own use. Each garage had a B-type lorry to fetch and carry spare parts. They would also carry the mechanics out to broken down buses, and if they could not repair them on the spot, tow them back. A number of vans were also built on B-type chassis to carry tickets round to the garages for distribution. As mentioned in Chapter 1, the Private Hire Department of the LGOC had already become involved in the transport of troops by bus, beginning with the Shoeburyness run of December 1908. It became common for buses to be hired to carry the Territorials and their baggage to their annual summer camps. The Household Cavalry Museum at Windsor even have photographs of Life Guards in full dress, polished cuirasses, plumed helmets and all, being transported by bus to the Royal Tournament.

Lieutenant Colonel H James of the Royal Army Medical Corps obtained permission from the LGOC in 1910, to investigate the potential of a B-type bus for use as an ambulance. In a paper for the *Journal of the Royal Army Medical Corps*, he described how, with the minimum of alteration, the vehicle could be adapted to carry four stretcher cases inside the lower deck, with room for an attendant and another sitting wounded man and nine seated wounded on the top deck. Lieutenant Colonel James had loading trials conducted and found that the task was much easier if the stair rail was removed. This job could be easily done with a spanner.[1]

In 1898 the War Office had introduced their War Subvention Scheme, whereby a firm which purchased a lorry of an approved pattern could obtain a subsidy, which, by 1914, totalled £110 for each vehicle. The scheme was updated following an unsatisfactory exercise in 1913, in which a very mixed bag of hired lorries was used. They included some very old ex-bus vehicles, old

Above
B-types at the Bank
Intersection, 1910
1998/45364

Above
B-type lorry at North Road,
assigned to Forest Gate garage.
2013/10825

Motor Omnibus Company, Straker and Büssing lorries.
Commercial Motor had its usual cogent comments to
make 'That old and practically worn-out chassis which
have seen many years service in London bus works should
find a place in these supply columns is undesirable'.[2]
In return for the subsidy, the civilian owner had to keep
the vehicle in good order (which was checked by regular
inspection) and had to surrender the vehicle to the
Army in time of war at the market price plus 25%.
This gave the Army access to a large transport fleet
without having to spend a lot of money from a
traditionally mean peacetime budget to buy and maintain
them. The B-type bus did not conform to the highly
detailed 1913 Subsidy lorry specifications but could
quickly be converted into a 3-ton lorry. The large fleet
of standardized B-type vehicles meant that, from 1913,
the B-type was recognised as eligible for the Subsidy
payments and buses from B2360 onwards were liable for
service. The LGOC Board or Directors were probably very
grateful they had taken the money as, on the outbreak
of the conflict in 1914, Minister of War Lord Kitchener
immediately requisitioned all available Subsidy vehicles
whether the payments had been made or not, as well as
large numbers of non-Subsidy lorries.

1   Lieutenant Colonel H E R James RAMC (Rtd). 'Adaptation of
    Motor Omnibus and Scotch Haycart for Carriage of Wounded
    Men' in *Journal of the Royal Army Medical Corps*, Vol. 15, 1910.

2   *Commercial Motor*, 2 October 1913

I envy not the rich and great,
A wandering minstrel, poor and free,
I am contented with my fate,
An omnibus suffices me.

Ballad of an Omnibus
Amy Levy (1861–1889)

SINGLE DECK BUS AMBULANCES OF THE ROYAL NAVY, 1914–1918

In October 1912 the London General Omnibus Company wished to replace a horse bus route through the Blackwall Tunnel with motor buses. For safety reasons, these had to be of single deck design. Initially a cut down version of the double deck B-type was used, with seating for sixteen passengers. This was found to be an uneconomic proposition, so a prototype 'bentwood' body, slightly wider than the standard version of the B-type bus, was fitted to the chassis of vehicle B1394.[1] The modification allowed two rows of three forward facing double seats separated by a central gangway at the front of the bus, with a four-seater bench lengthwise at the back on each side over the wheel arches. Twenty passengers could be seated. The single-deck buses were also required to run on routes such as that up Muswell Hill in north London, where there was a steep gradient and a low railway bridge. The chassis and the engine of the prototype proved to be too weak for the job, so thirty new stronger all-steel chassis (B2679 to B2708) were fitted with 40hp engines; they entered service in February 1914. The drivers, sitting in their open cabs, suffered from petrol fumes in the tunnel and were allowed a free pint of milk a day that was said to counteract the effects. They did not think it very effective!

On 1 August 1914, four days before war was declared, these almost brand-new passenger vehicles were the first London buses to be requisitioned for use by the Royal Navy as ambulances. Photographs give some indication of adaptations for the role.[2] The buses still appear to be in the bright red livery of the LGOC, with white painted window frames and the fleet name GENERAL in gold on each side. Destination boards on the roof were removed. To allow easier access for casualties on stretchers the rear platform and its rails were taken off. One reference says that the seats were removed and frames for stretchers installed. The large lower windows were obscured with white paint with a large red cross painted on one of the

Opposite
LGOC Charabanc-body B-type at Chatham as ambulance, 1914.
1998/83968

Above
Single deck B-type buses as ambulances, 1914.
1998/36874

Left
Casualties carried onto converted B-type ambulance B2701 at Plymouth.
2014/3834

windows, sometimes the front window and sometimes the second. Transparent advertisements remained visible in the small upper windows - a reminder of more peaceful times. One bus had a small white ensign flying from a small flagstaff fixed to the radiator cap. A photograph of B2696 (LH8145) shows a curtain attached to a wooden rail which could be drawn across the rear entrance to the bus to screen the wounded from the public gaze.[3]

The bus-ambulances seem to have served at naval ports. Photographs show B2703 (LH8152), B2704 (LH8153) and B2708 (LH8157) working at Plymouth. The Chief Constable of Plymouth wrote to the LGOC in November 1915 stating *'the LGOC drivers, who have been engaged in this Town for the past fourteen months working the large ambulances used for the Conveyance of wounded soldiers and sailors to and from the various hospitals, have carried out their work without my having received any complaint whatever as to their conduct or manner of driving, nor has there been any accident in connection therewith. I believe their work to have been done excellently'*.[4]

B2690, B2681, B2684 and B2698 were at Chatham and Devonport and remained in naval service even after the war ended. Only four of the single-decker ambulances (B2687, B2693, B2701 and B2705) returned to service on the streets of London after the conflict; all the rest were sold off to civilian operators. Their relatively easy service at home, on good roads and with regular maintenance must have made them bargains compared with the hard-used double-decker versions which returned from service in France and Belgium. James Weaver of the Southall and District Traction Company, ran three B-types with single deck bodies from January 1923 until April 1926. He bought B2687 (LH8036) direct from Devonport Docks and replaced the missing rear platform with a home-made extension of his own, which had to be removed again as it made the bus exceed the legal length.[5]

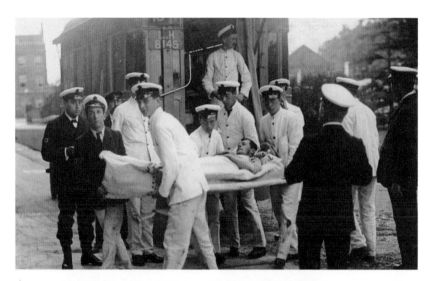

Top
B2696 converted to an ambulance.
2014/3835

Bottom
B2708 at Plymouth, whilst transporting Indian troops.
1998/36876

1   By steam heating ash frames under pressure, wood could
    be softened and bent into curved shapes over formers and
    retained its new shape on cooling. A passenger bus body was
    then fabricated over these frames.

2   On the 30 July the LGOC received a telegram asking for
    vehicles for the Navy as a matter of urgency. Within an hour
    Admiral Sir Arthur May had inspected several vehicles and
    chose the single deck B-types as most suitable. H E Blain and
    G J Shave - officials of the LGOC - were asked how long it
    would take to do the necessary work. '48 hours' they replied.
    The requisitioned buses were all called in to the North Road,
    Holloway, coach works. All the adaptations were completed
    in 26 hours and the buses left for service in Chatham, Dover
    and Plymouth. See 'The War Decorations of the London Bus',
    Commercial Motor, 24 February 1920, pp 20-22.

3   B numbers were the LGOC chassis and bonnet numbers for
    their buses. The number in brackets, for example (LH8145)
    is the registration number for the vehicle, in this case B2696.
    Both numbers are given in this book, as often only one of
    them is visible in a photograph.

4   *TOT* (*Train, Omnibus Tram*, the magazine of the Underground
    Group), Number 23, November 1915.

5   K C Blacker, R S Lunn and R G Westgate. *London's Buses:
    Volume One: The Independent Era 1922-1934*. St Albans:
    H J Publications, 1977, p 3. Blacker, Lunn and Westgate
    suggest Weaver built the bus bodies himself, with the help
    of a local carpenter.

And there was mounting in hot haste: the steed,
The mustering squadron and the clattering car,
Went pouring forth with impetuous speed,
And swiftly forming in the ranks of war;

Childe Harold's Pilgrimage, Canto the third.
George, Lord Byron (1788–1824)

DAIMLER BUSES OF THE ROYAL NAVY, 1914–1915

In the early years of the twentieth century the War Office had tried to keep all military aviation under its own control. Winston Churchill, who was First Lord of the Admiralty at this time, managed to keep a small naval aviation service by calling seaplanes 'flying boats'. He expanded this fleet later by adding some land planes, on the grounds they were needed to protect British naval bases from German Zeppelin airship attacks.

With the outbreak of war in August 1914, the army air service, the Royal Flying Corps (RFC), went to France with the British Expeditionary Force, leaving the naval aviators, the Royal Naval Air Service (RNAS), with the task of defending Britain from air attack.[1] This did not suit either Winston Churchill or his naval fliers who were keen to get involved with the action on the continent. It was quickly pointed out to Churchill that the primitive aircraft which the Navy flew were unable to climb to sufficient altitude to attack the Zeppelins, especially if they had to carry the weight of a machine gun as well as that of a pilot. The only way they could usefully attack the German airships was by bombing them in their sheds.

A small diversionary force of Royal Marines was landed at Ostend with instructions to act as if they were the vanguard of a major force. The Eastchurch squadron of the Royal Naval Air Service, under its charismatic commanding officer Lieutenant Commander Charles Rumney Samson (1883-1931), was sent to provide air reconnaissance for them. He had been one of the Navy's first pilots and had been the first British pilot to fly an aircraft from off a platform mounted on the turret of a battleship. On that occasion, he had been personally congratulated for his bravery by the German Kaiser, who was on one of His Imperial Majesty's pre-war visits to a British naval review. The Times of 23 November 1914 reported that the Kaiser had put a price of £1,000 on Samson's head for his wartime exploits, but that was after he had bombed Germany.

On 11 September 1914 Winston Churchill visited Dunkirk where French Chief of Staff Marshal Joseph Joffre asked him for help to provide a garrison for its defence. Churchill offered a brigade of Royal Marines. This was rather a grand term for a force of a few hundred recalled reservists. Lieutenant Commander Samson had been recalled from Ostend to England but reported that a fog in the Channel made it unsafe to fly back and landed instead at Dunkirk, where he quickly got the French commander to ask for his services. The force was joined by a regiment of Yeomanry (Territorial) cavalry the Queen's Own Oxfordshire Hussars, which included Winston's brother, John Strange 'Jack' Spencer-Churchill. Winston had also served in the regiment at one time along with other members of the family of the Duke of Marlborough.

To give the Marines more mobility, Major A H Ollivant RA, an army liaison officer at the Admiralty, suggested using London motor omnibuses as all other suitable vehicles had already been requisitioned by the War Office. He approached the London General Omnibus Company

Above
One of a number of lorries based on Daimler chassis built at the LGOC's works at North Road, Holloway, in 1914.
2004/8772

Opposite
Gearless Daimler D265 in the Grote Markt, Sint-Niklaas, Flanders, September 1914.
1998/83944

Left
MET Daimler with
disembarking troops
on the quayside at
Ostend, 1914.
1998/84320

Bottom left
MET Daimler buses,
in Sint-Niklaas,
Flanders, 1914.
1998/87642

Bottom right
RND armoured
Wolseley cars with
Daimler buses
in background,
Antwerp, 1914.
1998/84847

who made a call for volunteers from among their drivers. Large numbers of men came forward, and by the method of choosing the first three in alphabetical order from each garage, 70 two-man crews were selected. Such was the need for haste that, as soon as they had been sworn in as Royal Marines, they drove their buses from the Embankment to Dover, stopping on the way at the Royal Marine barracks at Chatham to be kitted out with uniforms. These were in short supply and most of the crews wore their civilian clothes with only one or two items of uniform such as a cap or a greatcoat.[2]

They were then shipped to Dunkirk under the command of Captain Wilfred Dumble of the Royal Engineers, who was made a temporary Royal Marine Lieutenant Colonel. Dumble was a Boer War veteran who had worked with Frank Searle for the Metropolitan Electric Tramways. The first batch of 20 buses arrived at Dunkirk on 24 September 1914 aboard the SS Erbswick Grange, and were unloaded the next day and parked in the Hangar de Commerce. The second group of 50 buses was due on 26 September but went to Calais on the SS Twickenham, as a submarine was reported at Dunkirk. A Captain Howard was sent to Calais to get the buses unloaded and moved to Dunkirk. Driver Robert Douglas went with him to help in the work. Transferring the vehicles was difficult because of the many trenches dug across the roads. Twenty two B-type lorries of the Army Service Corps were also put under the orders of Lieutenant Colonel Dumble.

The seventy buses chosen for this expedition were Daimler buses of the Metropolitan Electric Tramways (MET) and Gearless companies, who were both LGOC subsidiaries. Daimler buses were the only ones available, as the B-types were liable for Army service under the Subsidy scheme. There was no time to alter the Daimler buses in any way, so they carried their military passengers still in the blue and white colours of the MET and Gearless

companies, complete with destination boards and advertisements for Dewar's whisky and London shows.[3]

The War Diary of the Chatham (9th) Battalion Royal Marines records on 28 September 1914: 'Moved to Cassel and carried out operations in Motor-buses in conjunction with Armoured Cars in HAZEBROUCK area'.[4] On 1 October 1914, 35 buses under Captain Leaf went to Cassel and practised manoeuvres with parties of Royal Marines at Steenvorde to find out the best methods of using the buses. Marine Private A Doswell wrote to Underground group staff magazine TOT about this episode: 'at Cassel France – 7.30 am paraded and marched out as in action for about six miles. Then waited for MET omnibuses which took us for a joy ride – in reality a kind of raiding party, as Uhlans had been reported near, but we did not see any'.[5] Driver Robert Douglas also went on this trip but on his return to Cassel missed out on a place to sleep because he and his mate had gone off with the marines to scrounge some tea: they had to spend the night in their bus. Douglas was lucky and got issued a blanket, but his mate had only a borrowed officer's greatcoat to cover himself.

By 2 October the German advance through Belgium was threatening Antwerp. The only British troops immediately available to go to the help of the Belgian Army were the Royal Marine Brigade and the untrained Royal Naval Division. This was a force of Royal Naval Volunteer Reservists surplus to seagoing needs, which had been hastily armed with rifles and machine guns taken from the battleships of the Grand Fleet (the main fleet of the British Royal Navy during the First World War) where they were meant for the use of boarding parties. The Royal Marines were taken by bus to the railway station at Dunkirk from where they were moved by train to Antwerp. The 70 Daimler buses were sent in a convoy by road in support. So hurried was the move that the officers in command did not know the numbers of vehicles involved and no nominal roll of the men was available. There were also a number of staff cars provided by members of the Royal Automobile Club who had been commissioned as temporary Second Lieutenants in the Royal Marines. They were paid £1 a day and guaranteed compensation for damage to their cars.[6]

Escorted by eleven Wolseley armoured cars and two armoured B-type lorries of the Royal Naval Air Service, the convoy assembled on the airfield at Dunkirk. These last two vehicles had been crudely augmented by Samson at the Dunkirk foundry *Forge et Chantiers de France* with boiler plate armour which was more impressive than effective. The whole force was under the command of Lieutenant Commander Samson. A narrow corridor by way of Bruges and Ghent offered the only route still open to Antwerp. Ten Royal Marine riflemen rode on the top deck of every sixth bus acting as armed escort. No rations had been arranged for the drivers and Samson had to buy food for them himself at Belgian shops (one wonders if any of the drivers had been on the Shoeburyness run). All the way however they were given chocolate, fruit, tobacco and wine by the excited Belgian people: 'we had enough choc. etc thrown at us to stock a shop'.

Reaching Bruges at 23.00 on 3 October, the column spent the night in the barrack square, where for safety against possible German cavalry raids, all the buses were packed in so tightly that Captain Leaf, who commanded the bus column, did not believe that they could be extricated quickly. The expert London bus drivers had them all out and lined up on the road the next morning within twenty minutes of the order being given, ready to move off at 07.00. The Daimler buses, minus one which had broken down, entered Antwerp in a grand procession led by the armoured cars, to be handed over to the Royal Naval Division at the aviation ground.[7] 'We entered Antwerp

Left
Interior of MET Daimler bus D70 in use as a makeshift ambulance, Belgium, 1914.
1998/88850

Below
MET Daimler D70 again, arriving at Ghent with British troops wounded at Antwerp.
1998/84914

by crossing the [River] Scheldt over a pontoon bridge. It was a pantomime the bridge being scarcely wide enough for the buses and the weight making it sink and rise.' Their arrival was seen by American reporter Alexander Powell, who wrote '…their ammunition and supplies being brought by road, via Bruges and Ghent, in London motor-buses. When this procession of lumbering vehicles, placarded with advertisements of teas, tobaccos, whiskies and current theatrical attractions and bearing the signs 'Bank,' 'Holborn', 'Piccadilly', 'Shepherd's Bush', 'Strand,' rumbled through the streets of Antwerp, the populace went mad. The British had come at last! The city was saved. Vive les Anglais! Vive Tommy Atkins!'.[8]

The Daimlers were then detailed for transport and supply work and as ambulances. The 1st Brigade of the Royal Naval Division, for instance, which had four battalions named Collingwood, Hawke, Benbow and Drake, was given four buses carrying supplies. Instead of the buses being loaded with a mixed lot of stores, one bus for each battalion's needs, each bus was loaded with only one kind of equipment, so the buses had to be unloaded, the stores sorted, and then reloaded. Ivor Fraser, LGOC Advertising Manager, had gone to Antwerp with the Royal Naval Division and wrote on 13 October about the buses: 'I arrived back in England this afternoon, after a pretty strenuous ten days of it….The Motor Buses in Antwerp did a great work and all credit is due to the efficiency of the L.G.O. vehicles and their drivers; they absolutely kept the pot boiling the whole time by their incessant labour in feeding the trenches with ammunition and food, not to say the handling of the wounded. The coolness of the drivers under a veritable hell of shells and shrapnel fire was an outstanding feature and the fellow who had the good fortune to get through will have cause to be ever grateful for the manner our wonderful fleet assisted them. It was a sad sight to see our dear old MET Buses battered about by the roadside as we left them in our retirement'.[9]

The bus drivers were billeted in a girls' school with comfortable clean beds but they were shelled out of it on the morning of 8 October. The situation in Antwerp was becoming increasingly desperate, and the decision was made to withdraw on the 8th with the buses carrying wounded men. This was observed by Horace Green, the special correspondent of the *New York Evening Post*: 'that night and the next, loads of English Red Cross buses with their households of pain and ether rumbled over the pontoon bridge across the Scheldt, went past Fort Tête de Flandres and disappeared in the swampy meadows on the way to Ghent'.[10]

Mrs St. Clair Stobart, who had set up the British Women's Hospital in Antwerp after her services were refused by the War Office, went to look for transport to get away from the doomed city: 'It was like a bad dream. But suddenly I saw tearing along towards me, at breakneck pace, three London motor buses – a dream-like touch of incongruity. But I ran out into the road and, risking being run down, spread out my arms to stop them. Would they heed? Thank God they did, and I asked the drivers, English Tommies, if they could help me and my nurses to the frontier. 'If you're quick as lightning', they replied, 'but we have to get over the bridge of boats with our loads of ammunition, before it is blown up'. I ran back to the staff, and in a few minutes we had collected our handbags which were waiting piled up on the road, and were all seated, sixteen of us, on the boxes of ammunition inside those motor buses which tore along the streets, dodging or bumping in and out of great holes excavated by the shells. We laughed merrily at the thought of what fine fireworks we should be in the middle of, if a shell dropped our way'.[11]

H S Souttar FRCS, the surgeon in charge of what he called the Belgian Field Hospital, and which the Belgians persisted in calling the British Field Hospital, also went to look for transport to get out of the besieged city. He was promised six buses by General Paris, who commanded the British forces in Antwerp: '…and the buses were on the quay by the Arsenal at the extreme south end, so that we had to drive…a distance of about three miles… here was a long line of motor-buses, about sixty of them, all drawn up in a line along the river. Beside them was a long line of ammunition lorries, and on the other side was the Arsenal, on our left, blazing away, with a vast column of smoke lowering up to the sky. 'It may blow up at any minute,' said Colonel Farquarson cheerily, 'I had better move that ammunition.'…so we waited till the ammunition had been moved, and the Colonel had done his best to get us the motor-buses. He could only get four, so we had to make the best of a bad job.…At last we turned into our own street, the Boulevard Leopold, and there we met a sight which our eyes could scarcely credit. Three motor-buses stood before our door and patients were being crowded into them'.[12]

The anonymous author of *A War Nurse's Diary*, working in the same hospital, explains how they got there: 'One of our medical students had an uncle with Winston Churchill, so he just went round to Headquarters and borrowed three London Motor Omnibuses. These lumbering vehicles looked so incongruous still pasted with the latest music hall advertisements, such as 'The Glad Eye', the familiar 'Elephant & Castle' marking their original destination'.[13] The patients in the first three buses were sent off at once while the second batch of buses was filled with the remaining patients and the hospital equipment: 'Even at the last minute patients arrived, chiefly British. Just before we started a tall Marine in a navy jersey was helped in. He sat in the corner next to me. All his ribs were broken down one side, and he had no plaster or support. Opposite me were two Tommies with compound fractures of the leg. I placed both legs on my knees to lessen the jolting. The Marine suffered in silent agony, his lips pressed tightly together, and his white face set. I looked at him helplessly, and he said "Never mind me, Sister; if I swear don't take any notice". Fortunately they had pushed in two bottles of whiskey and some soda-syphons; I just dosed them all around until it was finished. Placing the Marine's arm around my shoulders, I used my right arm as a splint to support his ribs, and so we sat for seven and a half hours without moving'.[14]

By this time the only way out of Antwerp was by two pontoon bridges over the River Scheldt. The column of buses had to wait in the Cathedral Square for their turn to cross: 'At last there was a movement forwards; we crept down the slope and onto the bridge, and slowly moved over to the other side'.[15] The perils of crossing one of these bridges were described in the *Daily Chronicle* by a Royal Marine officer: 'Crossing the pontoon bridge from Antwerp they took no thought for their personal safety. They only had two inches of space on either side and the bridge rolled like a switchback, so some of the men on board leapt to their feet ready to jump into the water, but the drivers never made a mistake'.[16]

The bus carrying four women doctors from Mrs St. Clair Stobart's Hospital, was the last one over the lower pontoon ridge before it was blown up a few seconds later.[17] Mrs St. Clair Stobart herself remained behind to be captured by the Germans and was accused of being a spy, but she escaped the threatened firing squad to be repatriated, and then go with her hospital to serve in Serbia for the rest of the war. The Duchess of Sutherland, who was running another British hospital of her own in Brussels, simply informed the German officer who took her prisoner, that she was Millicent, Duchess of Sutherland and demanded repatriation as a non-combatant. She also told him she was a personal friend of the German Empress. She and her staff were put onto a motor-charabanc and sent to Holland.

Above
MET Daimler
captured in Ghent,
Belgium by the
German army.
1998/3659/

Major Olliphant, now promoted to Lieutenant Colonel, who had arrived to take charge of the transport, waited at the upper pontoon Bridge but was incapacitated by a kick on the head from a horse, which rendered him unconscious for several hours. Orders went astray and many men of the Royal Naval Division went to the wrong bridge after it had been destroyed and had to cross in small boats. They had little food and water but found a broken down bus partly loaded with some ships' biscuits at St. Gillaes Waes station near Antwerp. 'We made as many journeys as we possibly could to & from a small station to entrain for Ostend. We had as many as 60 or 70 marines on the car at one time & made four or five journeys'. Finally, cut off by the German Army, some were captured and others, including one bus driver, entered neutral Holland, to be interned by the Dutch for the duration of the war. The remaining buses had been withdrawn by way of the Tête de Flandres, St. Nicholas and St. Gillaes Waes. Rupert Brooke, the war poet and Sub-Lieutenant in the Anson battalion of the Royal Naval Division, wrote of seeing the buses there: 'The refugees and motor-buses and transport and Belgian troops grew thicker. After about a thousand years it was dawn. The motor-buses indicated that we were bound for Hammersmith and might be allowed to see *Potash and Perlmutter*'.[18]

Dr Souttar added: 'We reached St. Nicholas about eight o'clock, having covered thirteen miles in three hours. It was quite dark, and as we had a long night before us we decided to stop and get some food for ourselves and our patients. There was not much to be had, but it was wonderful there was anything. We now hoped to push on faster, and to reach Ghent before midnight, for it is only a little over twenty miles by the direct road. To our dismay we found that Lokeren, half-way to Ghent was in the hands of the Germans, and that we must make a detour, taking us close to the Dutch border, and nearly doubling the distance'.[19]

In the early hours of 9 October the bus column was ordered to Selzaete for petrol and orders: 'These were minor roads, with a narrow paved causeway in the centre, and loose sand on either side. Long avenues of trees kept us in inky darkness, and how the drivers succeeded in keeping on the causeway I really do not know. Every now and then one of the buses would get into the sand; then all the men would collect, dig the wheels clear, and by sheer brute force drag the bus back to safety. Twice it seemed absolutely hopeless. The wheels were in the loose sand within a foot of a deep ditch, and the least thing would have sent the bus flying into the field beyond; and on both occasions a team of huge Flemish horses appeared from nowhere in the darkness and dragged us clear'.[20]

Our anonymous war nurse gives further account of the escape from Antwerp: 'How can I ever describe that journey to Ghent of fourteen and a half hours? No one but those who went through it can realize it. Have you ever ridden in a London motor bus? To begin with, even traversing the smooth London streets these vehicles jolt you to bits, whilst the smell of burnt gasoline is often stifling, so just imagine these unwieldy things bumping along over cobble stones and the loose sandy ruts of rough tracks among the sand-dunes, which constantly necessitated everyone who could, dismounting and pushing behind and pulling ropes in front, to get the vehicles out of the ruts. When you have this picture before you, just think of the passengers — not healthy people on a penny bus ride, but wounded soldiers and sailors. All those inside passengers were either wounded in the abdomen, shot through the lungs, or pierced through the skull…whilst we had more than one case of men with broken backs. Many of these had been operated on…For twenty-four hours these men had had no nourishment and we were so placed that it was impossible to reach them…very soon all the ills that could happen to sick men came upon us. The jolting and

Left
French postcard
showing a MET
Daimler bus with
wounded soldiers
and nurses at Ghent,
1914.
2013/12308

agony made them very sick. Seizing any utensil which had been saved from the theatre I gave It to them.'[21]

Dr Alice Benham, one of the female doctors from the British Field Hospital, reported her experiences at a meeting of the Association of Registered Medical Women on 10 November 1914 under the title of *A month spent in Antwerp with the British Field Hospital*: 'The staff consisted of four women and three men doctors and fourteen trained nurses; later they were joined by several more nurses and a surgeon from a London hospital. A large school was converted into a hospital with about 150 beds, and a few days after their arrival 140 wounded were admitted In one day. Many were collapsed…several required immediate operation, for instance, four abdominal cases, several depressed fractures of the skull, one excision of an eye – and all did very well…Fourteen hours after bombardment

commenced the patients were removed in seven motor ambulances to Ghent. One died on the way and one after arrival…During the month 400 wounded were treated at the hospital, forty English and the rest Belgians'.[22]

Six buses had to be abandoned for lack of petrol at Selsaete, Belgium, and others were lost due to mechanical defects so several buses had to be left for the Germans to collect as booty. One was rescued by Dr Albert De Moor of the Belgian Army who got it going, with difficulty, as later it was found the engine cylinder had split and had been welded as a repair. He and his drivers got six other buses mobile but were ordered to send them to Selsaete station and they were never seen again:

'At Selsaete, only a mile from the Dutch border, we turned southwards towards Ghent, and for an interminable

Above

The 1st Cameronians on MET Daimlers still in their original livery. The original photo is black and white but the printer has added the wrong colour. At this stage the buses would have been blue, not green. The French publisher also changed the side advert from Dewar's whisky to Dubonnet! The photo was taken by Lieutenant (later Major General) Robin Money, on the road from Vlamertinghe to Laventie, 19 October 1914. It is thought that several of the Cameronians officers were allowed to carry cameras, contrary to regulations, so their photographs featured a lot in the early war media. Lieutenant Money sent his films home and his father sold the pictures to various papers and magazines.
1998/65183, 2004/9686

Right

Royal Naval Division Daimlers at Boulogne, 1914.
1998/83862

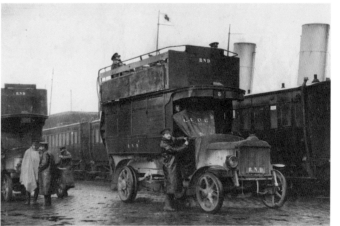

distance we followed the bank of a large canal. A few miles from Ghent we met Lieutenant Commander Samson, of the Flying Corps, and three of his armoured cars. The blaze of their headlights quite blinded us after the darkness in which we had travelled, but the sight of British uniforms and the machine guns was a great encouragement. The road was so narrow that they had to turn their cars into a field to let us pass. ...the grey armoured cars, with their blazing headlights, and our four red motor-buses made a strange scene.[23] At last we reached Ghent utterly tired out, though personally I had slept a sort of night-mare sleep on the top step of the bus which boldly announced its destination as Hendon. It was five o'clock and day was breaking as we got our patients out of the buses and deposited them in the various hospitals as we could find room for them. To our unspeakable relief, we found that the rest of our party had come through by much the same road, but they had reached Ghent quite early the night before. Their earlier start had given them the advantage of clearer roads and daylight...and we hoped our troubles were over. Alas! We were told that the Germans were expected to enter Ghent that very day, and that all British wounded must be removed from the hospitals before ten o'clock. There was nothing for it but to collect them again, and take them to Ostend. One had died in the night, and two were too ill to be moved. We left them behind in skilled hands, and the others we re-embarked on our buses en route for Bruges and Ostend.'[24]

The vehicles finally reached Bruges at 20.30, obtained petrol and left for Blankenberge and Ostend. Driver Roberts wrote 'having been on the bus from Thursday morning to Friday night. Did not wait for supper, rolled in blankets & slept till 6 am'. Royal Marine driver T J Acteson met some old friends on the road, as he later wrote to TOT: 'I met two of my old chums from Forest Gate, in Drivers Golding and Tonquett, making their way out of

Antwerp as best they could, loaded with ammunition and stores, with the 'diff' an inch or two off the ground'.[25] At Ostend the main column joined up with the small group that had left Selsaete, under the command of Lieutenant Churchyard, a short time earlier. After spending the night at Ostend they returned to Dunkirk. Driver Roberts records fitting his bus with wooden windows on the 14th of October.

At Dunkirk they found themselves 'nobody's children' as the Royal Naval Division had returned to England, until Winston Churchill lent them to the army.[26] Of the Daimlers, 46 buses and 23 lorries were sent to St. Omer on 15 October 1914. They were joined by 50 lorries of the Royal Marine Artillery batteries on 17 October. Because the unit had no repair lorry or tools, a garage was taken over in the Rue de Strasbourg at St. Omer at a cost of 100 francs a week for the use of the premises and all its machines. This was put under the command of Captain Leaf, who was eventually awarded the DSO for his services.[27]

The buses were joined by a number of army vehicles but there was some friction when the army drivers found that they were being paid only six shillings a day, whilst the Royal Marine drivers were being paid ten shillings a day. They were involved in transporting troops for the First Battle of Ypres in October and November 1914, including the Cameronians and the Argylls on 19 October. Also amongst these troops were the 57th Punjab regiment of the Lahore Division of the Indian Army, moved on 22 October. Daimler buses conveyed detachments from various units to take part in the funeral of Lord Roberts, who had died of pneumonia whilst visiting Indian troops in France.

On 1 November 1914 Captain Howard was sent to recover three buses and a lorry that had been sent to

Ypres, under the command of Sergeant Major Alfred Chouffot, for use as regimental transport by the London Scottish. Sergeant Major Chouffot, who in peacetime had been an inspector for the LGOC, complained to Captain Howard that the buses had been heavily overloaded, and that they had been sent out without his consent. (Sergeant Major Chouffot was eventually awarded the DSM for his work.) Captain Howard insisted that the buses must be returned the next day to Bailleul. The next chapter will tell what happened to them. In November 1914 the Daimlers were painted dark green and given white letters RND on the front and side to denote the Royal Naval Division.[28]

A number of buses were used from time to time to take leave parties to and from Boulogne and during this service bus 35 went off the road when its steering went and overturned with 8 officers on board. The bus was recovered by a party of the ASC with a steam traction engine and, after righting the vehicle and replacing the front axle, the bus was driven back to St. Omer under its own power. Another accident occurred on 1 February 1915 when a bus, which had become ditched, had to be overturned to let the rest of the convoy, carrying men of the Yorkshire Light Infantry, pass near Reninghelst. Horse transport had been allowed on to a road reserved for a long column of the buses of the RND and the 1st Auxiliary Omnibus Coy, and the convoy had to be turned by backing down a side road, waiting for two hours, and then travelling on a less suitable road. On 6 February 1915 Captain Howard returned to England to resume his parliamentary duties as Liberal Chief Whip leaving Captain Leaf in command.

The first Royal Marine 15inch Howitzer (called 'Granny') arrived at Boulogne on 18 and 19 February 1915, and six buses transported the crews. On 2 April they went to Bailleul to carry the Artists' Rifles to St. Omer to become the General Headquarters Guard. During the Second Battle of Ypres they carried troops under fire from Hazebrouck and Vlamertinghe and on 19 April they brought back 800 wounded. By August 1915 the decision was made for the army to take over the Royal Marine Transport Company and make it part of the Army Service Corps. The NCOs and men were given the option of staying on, at the lower army rates of pay, as the 16th Auxiliary Omnibus Coy, or transferring to other Royal Marine units. Most of them preferred to transfer and went as drivers to the Royal Marine Artillery Howitzer and Anti-Aircraft Brigades.

Daimler buses continued to serve in France and Belgium during the war. By November 1918, 113 Daimler buses were still in military service including the 46 London Daimlers surviving the Antwerp siege, many more had been converted into lorries. The City of Manchester, for example, lost six of its eight Daimler buses (on loan from the MET) which were required as lorries, but it was able to use the stored bodies again later in the war, when new Daimler chassis became available. Any Daimler vehicle was liable for impressment and one bus company hid theirs to avoid this fate. A Daimler bus which had been sold to Vienna in 1913 and driven across Europe for delivery, was requisitioned by the Austro-Hungarian army and served with them during the war. This was one of a number of vehicles that had been sold abroad, mostly to New York. They had left hand staircases but retained the right hand drive.

1   The Royal Flying Corps was in existence from 1912 to 1918. The Royal Naval Air Service was created in 1914, and merged with the Royal Flying Corps to create the Royal Air Force in 1918.

2   Robert Douglas records being issued with his first uniform items on 14 October 1914 – two pairs of socks, two shirts and one pair of boots. He did not get his next issue until 13 November: more boots, holdall, rifle and webbing, and his first army cap.

3   George Robbins. *Metropolitan: the story of The Tramways (MET) Omnibus Company Limited 1912-1933*. London: Omnibus Society Publication, 1977

4   War Diary, Chatham Battalion (9th) Royal Marines. National Archives reference WO95/3108.

5   *TOT*, 14 November 1914, p2. 'Uhlan' was a type of German cavalry soldier.

6   Charles Rumney Samson. *Fights and Flights*. London: Ernest Benn, 1930.

7   Charles Rumney Samson. *Fights and Flights*. London: Ernest Benn, 1930.

8   Alexander E Powell. *Fighting in Flanders*. London: William Heinemann, 1915.

9   Ivor Fraser, Notes on News, *TOT*, 17 October 1914, p1.

10 Horace Green. *The Diary of a Non-Combatant*. Boston: Houghton & Mifflins Co, 1915.

11 Mabel Annie St Clair Stobart. *Miracles and Adventures: an autobiography*, n p: Rider, 1935.

12 H S Souttar FRCS. *A Surgeon in Belgium*. London: Edward Arnold, 1915.

13 Anon. *A War Nurse's Diary: sketches from a Belgian field hospital*. New York: The Macmillan Company, 1918.

14 Anon. *A War Nurse's Diary: sketches from a Belgian field hospital*. New York: The Macmillan Company, 1918.

15 H S Souttar FRCS. *A Surgeon in Belgium*. London: Edward Arnold, 1915.

16 *Daily Chronicle* quoted in TOT, 9 January 1915, p3.

17 The personnel were Dr. Helen Hanson, Dr. Mabel Ramsey, Dr. Florence Stoney and Dr. Joan Watts.

18 *The Collected Poems of Rupert Brooke: with a Memoir* (by Edward Marsh). London: Sidgwick & Jackson, 1918, cxxxi. The buses still carried their London destination and adverts. In 1914 the Jewish comedy *Potash and Perlmutter* by Montague Glass played at the Queen's Theatre, Shaftesbury Avenue, London.

19 H S Souttar FRCS. *A Surgeon in Belgium*. London: Edward Arnold, 1915.

20 H S Souttar FRCS. *A Surgeon in Belgium*. London: Edward Arnold, 1915.

21 Anon. *A War Nurse's Diary: sketches from a Belgian field hospital*. New York: The Macmillan Company, 1918.

22 Dr. Alice Benham, in *The British Medical Journal*, 28 November 1914, p.922.

23 Only blue MET and GEARLESS buses went to Antwerp. This may be either an example of poor colour memory or perhaps red/green colour blindness in Mr. Souttar. It might just be the mistake of a sub-editor who only knew of red London buses.

24 H S Souttar FRCS. *A Surgeon in Belgium*. London: Edward Arnold, 1915.

25 T J Acteson, 'A Busy Marine', *TOT*, April 1915, p2

26 General Sir H E Blumberg. *Britain's Sea Soldiers, 1914-1919*, n.p.: Swiss & Co, 1927

27 It may be seen with Captain Leaf's other medals at the Royal Marines Museum, Southsea, Hampshire.

28 Driver Robert Douglas records painting his bus green on 29 October and 3 November 1914.

But that's all shove be'ind me
— long ago an' fur away.
An' there ain't no 'busses running
from the Bank to Mandalay

Mandalay, Rudyard Kipling (1865–1936)

MILITARY B-TYPE BUSES, 1914–1919

Kipling may not have seen London buses in Burma but they were soon to appear in many places abroad. On 18 September 1914, the War Office put out an urgent call for more buses to supplement the Daimlers of the Royal Navy. This time 300 B-types were requisitioned. Half of them had their bus bodies removed and put into store so the chassis could be converted into lorries, whilst the other 150 were sent to France still in their red paint. When the Royal Navy had asked for volunteers to man their Daimler buses far more came forward than could be used at that time. Lists of the volunteers had been kept, however, and many men were surprised on turning up for that day's work to be told they were to become soldiers the next day. After being paid off by the LGOC they were entrained to the army motor transport depot which had been set up at Grove Park in south-east London, where a workhouse infirmary – Grove Park Hospital – had been requisitioned as an Army Service Corps barracks.

There they became soldiers in the Corps. Each driver was allowed to pick his partner 'as you may be together for some time'.[1] The London General Omnibus Company had a policy before the war of employing ex-servicemen and some of these old soldiers were appointed as NCOs. Driver Lewis records that both the section sergeants of the 1st Auxiliary Omnibus Coy wore the ribbons of the South Africa Medal. Although uniforms were issued, some items, such as cap badges were in short supply and many drivers continued to wear their General cap badges for as long as they could get away with it. Their first job was to requisition their vehicles: 'We were given lunch and ordered to parade after the meal, this time in uniform. Then we were formed into groups being sent to a London Bus Garage, and as a bus entered the garage, so two of us would take it over, and then we formed a convoy, and drove the buses back to Grove Park, where we parked in the street for the night.'[2]

The men were formed into Army Service Corps Mechanical Transport units. The first was the 1st Auxiliary Omnibus Coy with 75 buses, and the second was the 2nd Auxiliary Omnibus Coy with the other 75 buses. Two other units were formed at this time: the 3rd Auxiliary Omnibus Coy and 4th Auxiliary Omnibus Coy, each with 75 lorries converted from B-type buses. They became Divisional Ammunition Columns. The busmen were never allocated sleeping quarters, because of the constant need for mobility. They had to live in their vehicles, with personal belongings stowed in wooden boxes and old petrol tins, in any convenient place they could find on the bus. The men were never off duty, drivers being either out on work details or on standby for new orders. Driver Lewis records that he and his mate slept in the back of their lorry, he on a home-made hammock, his mate on the driver's seat removed from the cab, (sleeping on the seats was a failure as they were so narrow they fell off every time they turned over).[3] If a call came in the night, they would hurriedly dress, and whilst one driver drove off, the other would pack their gear away as best he could in the darkness. Lewis and his mate Hindmarsh, each had one side of the lorry with a padlocked box under the seat for their gear plus a kitbag for their clothes which could be secured by a lockable bar which went through the eyelets in the top of the kitbag. They had a food box which needed careful packing to prevent everything being shaken up by the vibration of the bus on the road, so that cocoa, sugar and petrol from the Primus stove (there was no source of paraffin available) did not end up together. (The vibration slowly destroyed his wrist-watch as it lost in turn its glass, second, minute and hour hands – at which point he got a pocket watch.) There was also the vehicle's tool-box, although each driver kept his own magneto spanner on his person because they were too valuable to let out of their sight. Despite all their precautions Lewis noted with some feeling 'In my experience the only troops who were not thieving bastards were the Guards'.[4] The boot

Opposite
Wounded troops board a B-type at the Front in freezing winter conditions.
1998/38988

could be on the other foot sometimes. William Mahoney tells of the fate of six bottles of cherry brandy, which had been left on his bus by mistake by a colonel of the Ox and Bucks Light Infantry, all of which were drunk by his fellow driver who was found under a bus semi-comatose and muttering 'lubricate, lubricate'.

The primitive living conditions cannot have been very restful, especially on cold winter nights when, in the absence of anti-freeze (Robert Douglas records using methylated spirit as a form of anti-freeze on 20 November 1914), it was necessary to get up every two hours, crank the starting handle to fire the engine and then run it for a while to heat up the water in the radiator so that it would not freeze and crack the engine block or split the radiator. The usual system was for two men to start at one end of a row of buses and start them up, leave them running and move on to the next. By the time they had reached the end of the row they and the buses were well warmed up and they would go back and switch the engines off starting with the first. They could then retire for the night knowing it was some other poor devils' turn in two hours time. Driver Lewis said that the only time he ever lit the oil lamps on his lorry was to put one under the bonnet on cold Continental winter's nights to keep the engine warm. Despite all these precautions most of the 1st Auxiliary Omnibus Coy's buses suffered from frost damaged radiators in the extremely cold winter of 1916/17.

Drivers were expected to maintain their own vehicles, and such was the reliability of the B-type design that many received no base workshop overhaul throughout the war. However tired a crew was on returning from a detail they had first to check water, petrol, grease, oil and undertake mechanical maintenance before they could turn in. The lower deck windows were found to be broken rather easily by troops wearing full packs so they were removed

and the openings boarded up with wooden planks. William Mahoney relates how, in June 1916, when his bus was being fitted with a new differential, his mate Charles pasted fresh newspapers up inside their bus, number 20, to make it more homely and seal some of the draughts.

Often, in the early days of the war, the buses were the only motor vehicles available and so had to carry troops, rations, ammunition or wounded, whatever might be needed. Once more lorries had arrived the buses were reserved for troop transport. 1,319 B-Type vehicles served in France and Belgium during the War and immediately afterwards. Requisitioned buses and lorries from the LGOC totalled 954, including converted from buses. The others were produced from new by the AEC, mostly as lorries. An unrecorded number of buses were sent further afield. Private C J Noyes, an ex-LGOC driver, wrote about seeing B-types at Salonika, Greece, in the June 1917 issue of TOT. Ishobel Ross, a cook with the Scottish Women's Hospitals America Unit, wrote in her diary of the transfer of her hospital from Mikra Bay, near Salonika to Lake Ostrovo, near the Serbian border. They had a very difficult journey. She finally got through to their destination in an ambulance car to find nothing ready for them and they had to sleep, packed like sardines, in the few tents available:

'5 September [1916]
The most exciting day I have ever spent! I was up at 4 am to get the tea on, and we filed out of camp about 7 am The convoy consisted of about 37 motor buses with about 12 yards between each......... The roads are not bad in this area as they had been remade by the Allies since the start of the war, but they got worse and worse as we went on....The remainder of the convoy will probably have to spend the night at the roadside."
'6 September,The others have been coming in all morning; they had to halt at nightfall, and sleep in their buses.'[5]

Top
The Army Service
Corps Barracks at
Grove Park.
*Michael Young
collection*

Bottom
Buses at Grove Park,
1914.
*Michael Young
collection*

Above
ASC drivers receive training from an LGOC man, at Grove Park.
1998/36584

Right
Photograph sent by a driver in Salonika to the *Daily Mirror*, showing his
bus B2411 with a donkey foal standing on the bonnet. The donkey,
called Tiny, was found by the roadside and became the mascot of the
26th Divisional Train.
1998/36626

Private Trenbath of the Royal Army Medical Corps, was to meet the buses further south when his draft was transported from Itea, a small port on the Gulf of Corinth, to Larisa where they could get a train to Salonika: 'February 19th [1918] – Certainly we got little rest at Itea, and we were all fixed up in buses by 9 o'clock – 23 buses composed the convoy. We travelled up one mountain to a height of 9,000 ft, going backwards and forwards by hair-pin bends, across one side of it. I counted 10 laps! It took us a little over four hours to ascend one side of the mountain and come down the other'.[6]

After the war it would have been too costly to repatriate these vehicles and several were bought to provide a bus service in Athens. The open upper deck on at least one bus was fitted with an awning to counter the fierce Greek sun.

At this point it is useful to consider the war experiences of each Auxiliary Omnibus Company in detail.

1st Auxiliary Omnibus Company

The 1st Auxiliary Omnibus Coy left Grove Park on 17 October 1914 with a column of 4 motor cars, 75 motor buses and 1 workshop lorry under the command of Major Morrison. It travelled down the Great West Road, reaching Marlborough on the first day via Reading. On 18 October the Company set off for Avonmouth, the port for Bristol. This port had a new facility in the Royal Edward Dock, constructed four years previously with some of the few cranes in the country large enough to lift vehicles onto ships. It therefore became the departure point for most motor transport. So many vehicles got lost in Bristol looking for Avonmouth that large new signs had to be hurriedly erected to show the route. On the second day of the move, the workshop lorry broke down and had to be left behind. The 1st Auxiliary Omnibus Coy sailed on several ships, including the S S Eddystone, around the coast of western England, across the English Channel,

and up the River Seine to Rouen, which again was a port with large cranes that could cope with the buses. At Rouen the Coy was given a replacement lorry. On 23 October they left Rouen for Blangy and the next day went forward to St. Omer to join the Second Army. One bus was lost on the way due to a collision with a wall.

These buses were still in their red livery, and a surprised reporter met them on a dusty road in France: 'The first bus rumbled past with a 'toot-toot'; it was a No. 8 Red General. A score swung by, all full inside and out. The last, a lingerer, bore the magic word 'Cricklewood' upon the backboard and the conductor spying me, half smothered in the dust, rang the bell, and sang out, "Here you are sir, Charing Cross, Saint Paul's – nip on, there ain't nobody looking". "Where are you bound for?" I asked...."A place called Crécy, sir, wherever that may be. Have you heard of it? Is there a pub there?". "Only a windmill, so far as I can remember", I answered'.[7]

The first troop transport was performed on 25 October when 22 officers and 600 men of the Seaforth Highlanders were carried in 3 cars, 40 buses and 1 lorry. On 29 October 1914, the 1st Auxiliary Omnibus Coy conveyed 28 officers and 750 men of the London Scottish, including the future film star Ronald Coleman, to the First Battle of Ypres. They were the first Territorial regiment in France and were hastily gathered up from their duties on the lines of communication to reinforce the thinning ranks of the Regular Army, which had been transferred from the Aisne to Ypres, partly by a fleet of borrowed French buses. One car and thirty five buses moved the battalion from St. Omer to Ypres. It was pouring with rain and the journey was miserable especially for those on the open top deck. One of the London Scottish, Baxter Milne described the journey: 'the road was abominable and we travelled without lights. Our particular bus was ditched four times, which meant we all got out and pushed. The other buses did not fare much better, but we all helped each other.'[8]

On arrival they were marched and counter-marched to plug gaps as each new German threat appeared. Buses took the London Scottish from Ypres to St. Eloi on 30 October, to reinforce General Gough's Cavalry Division on the Messines ridge. For their first-line horse-drawn transport the London Scottish were given that of the 1st Battalion, Coldstream Guards. When their colonel asked what the Coldstreams would use he was told that the transport section was virtually all that was left of that battalion. As no second-line motor transport, had been provided Captain Webb, the quartermaster of the London Scottish, kept three of the buses 'which he retained with admirable firmness in the face of repeated demands for their return'.[9] These three buses were the missing Daimlers of the Royal Marine Transport Company that we read about in the previous chapter. The London Scottish made a famous bayonet charge in which they suffered fifty per cent casualties. Private Ronald Coleman sustained a shell wound to his ankle, which finished his army career. Two buses were lost to heavy shell-fire at St. Eloi. One of these buses was trapped between the opposing lines, and despite attempts at retrieval, it had to be abandoned. The story was reported in TOT in December 1915 drawing on a letter from army private S T Cann, accompanied by an image credited to the *Daily Mirror*. TOT reported that the bus went out with the 90 Coy from Grove Park on the 17 October 1914 and was believed to be the one lost by Driver Rolls on the 28 October that year.

The site of the action is easily recognised today because the farm alongside it became known as *Bus House* and the Bus House Military Cemetery is still there. The busmen had to fight their way out of several small skirmishes, and one proudly bore his prisoners back on the upper deck with the rails adorned by German spiked helmets. Buses remained in their red livery for a few weeks, when each crew was given a tin of paint and told to paint their bus khaki, with white numbers and unit signs. By the end of 1914 the 1st Auxiliary Omnibus Coy had carried 15,698 men and travelled 3022 miles in convoy.

Driver Lewis joined the 1st Auxiliary Omnibus Coy in 1917 as an army-trained driver when the Auxiliary (Omnibus) Park MT was formed at Saint-Valery-sur-Somme, Picardie.[10] In his record of the war, he described the high quality of his Army Service Corps comrades. Most of them were teetotal as the LGOC would instantly sack any driver who smelt of alcohol when he arrived for work. This enabled Lewis to draw both his own and his mate's rum ration. Former LGOC personnel also did not smoke on duty. Many were older men in their forties and fifties and had sons serving in France. They only accepted Lewis when they found out that he was a volunteer and not a conscript.[11] (Lance Corporal Gower of the 16th Auxiliary Omnibus Coy recorded that the worst insult one of his driver pals could think of to call the cook, after a bad meal, was 'conscript.') By this time the company was commanded by Captain E H Allott, assisted by Sergeant Major Chouffot on his Douglas motorcycle. Each of the two bus sections was commanded by a First Lieutenant, assisted by a sergeant and a corporal. The two drivers on each vehicle were classified as first or second drivers and the seniority was decided by length of service – with the LGOC! Each first driver ranked as a Lance Corporal. Although the drivers occasionally got leave the services of the officers and sergeants were too important for them to be allowed to go.

2nd Auxiliary Omnibus Company

The 2nd Auxiliary Omnibus Coy left Grove Park on 22 October 1914 for Hampton Court. From photographs it would appear that the later Omnibus Coy buses were painted khaki before they left Grove Park.

Left
'London Bus Men'
of 1st Auxiliary
Bus Company (90
Company MT ASC).
2014/3838

Bottom left
Wrecked Daimler
bus at St Eloi, 1914.
1998/84919

Bottom right
Ex-LGOC Inspector
Alfred Chouffot,
pictured in TOT
February 1916, with
his Distinguished
Service Medal
awarded in January
1915 'for convoying
a column of
transport, frequently
under fire, in the
neighbourhood
of Ypres and
elsewhere',
2014/249

Left
The 2nd Auxiliary
Omnibus Company
(also known as the
91 Company).
1998/36517

The photographs show that the advertisements and the GENERAL signs on the side have gone. Two buses, B26 and B1779, fell out on the journey due to motor trouble. B1779 was repaired by the Catford depot and rejoined the column but B26 was left behind. The bad luck continued, as on the way to Avonmouth on 23 October B1321 was severely damaged when it collided with a lamp-post and had to be left in Bristol.

Under the command of Lieutenant S Janson, 4 officers and 189 men, with 3 cars, 73 buses, 1 lorry and 6 motor cycles, sailed in three ships, the *SS Trevanion*, the *SS Woodfield* and the *SS Treverbyn*. The first two ships arrived in Rouen on 27 October, but the *SS Treverbyn* was delayed for two days because it had to take on coal

at Barry. On 30 October the 2nd Auxiliary Omnibus Coy moved from Rouen to Neufchatel, B349 and B1216 needing repairs en route because of more motor problems. The Coy came under the orders of the First Army and set up their headquarters near Steenevoorde. On 12 November they took 600 French soldiers and two mitrailleuses (a form of wheeled machine gun) of the 57th Battalion of Chasseurs Alpins from Bailleul to Dickebusch over terrible roads clogged by masses of cavalry and infantry. During this journey several buses had windows blown out by the concussion of artillery firing near them.

By the end of 1914 the 2nd Auxiliary Omnibus Coy had transported 200 officers, 9394 men and travelled 2,650 miles in convoy.[12]

3rd Auxiliary Omnibus Company/4 GHQ Ammunition Park (later 50th Auxiliary Omnibus Coy)

This company had been formed on October 1914 at Grove Park, using B-type bus chassis converted to lorries. Its work as an Ammunition Park transporting artillery supplies, is outside our terms of reference but in December 1916, on the formation of the Auxiliary (Omnibus) Park at Saint-Valery-sur-Somme, the decision was made to convert its lorries back into troop carriers by fitting charabanc bodies; it then became the 50th Auxiliary Omnibus Coy. This was the Headquarters Company of the Auxiliary (Omnibus) Park, and for administrative purposes the independent sections of 25 buses that remained allocated to each of the Armies, as well as 82 converted lorries, were attached to it. The Auxiliary (Omnibus) Park will be described in Chapter 6.[13]

4th Auxiliary Omnibus Company

This company was formed 28 October 1914 at Grove Park. Unlike the other bus companies, the drivers of the 4th Auxiliary Omnibus Company were not LGOC personnel, but were described as specially enlisted men. Private 6948 F J Darby of the 46 Coy MT ASC wrote how he volunteered as a driver on 19 October 1914 because of a letter from his trade society, The Society of Automobile Mechanics, telling him of the urgent need for drivers for the Army. His comrades were a motley collection of bus, lorry, taxi and car drivers. One mate was even a tram driver with only a minimal knowledge of how to drive a bus.[14] (Perhaps this former tram driver was the one who drove Company Sergeant Major E Shephard of the 1st Dorsets on 4 December 1915: 'Caught a motor bus from Bray Church....Our driver evidently knew very little about his job. We stopped every time gear was changed'.)[15] It is likely the drivers of the 4th were much the same mixture. Their B-type buses were converted to lorries and any few remaining as buses were quickly fitted with lorry bodies. When the Auxiliary (Omnibus) Park M1

was formed in December 1916, 7 GHQ Ammunition Park (339 Coy ASC) became 51st Auxiliary Omnibus Company at Saint-Valery-sur-Somme, with 41 lorries and 54 buses. The Peerless lorries were converted to charabancs. On 19 March 1919 a section of 6 charabancs under the command of Lance Corporal Coakes was sent to the Base Commandant at Antwerp for detached duty, putting the bus companies back where they had first started in 1914. The 51st Auxiliary Omnibus Company was demobilized far to the east at Cologne in May 1919.[16]

15th Auxiliary Omnibus Company

The 15th Auxiliary Omnibus Coy was formed in July 1915, at Bulford Camp, Wiltshire. The Company left Avonmouth Docks on 18 September, shipped on the SS Imperial Transport and the SS Glenduin. They recorded in their War Diary having to make and fit lamp brackets and petrol carriers to their vehicles and to provide pickaxes, shovels and buckets for each bus and charabanc.[17] Some of these charabancs were on American Locomobile (Riker) chassis. In February 1916 command of the company was taken over by Captain M Beattie as the previous commanding officer, Captain Benn, was under arrest, the War Diary does not give any more details. It does, however, list the workshop tasks for July 1916 when the number of vehicles needing repairs were:

Number of vehicles in for

General Overhaul	5
Engine repairs	55
Body repairs	16
Chassis repairs	38
New tyres	7
Back axle repairs	2
Radiator repairs	13

In February 1917 the 15th Auxiliary Omnibus Coy was at Frévent, Nord-Pas-de-Calais, where the War Diary records that it transferred 25 Locomobile buses to the 50th Auxiliary Omnibus Coy to make the Third Army bus section up to strength. The only details of these vehicles comes from four photographs which seem to show spare bus bodies mounted on Locomobile chassis. One rather poor quality photograph from the Tank Museum collection shows a row of buses with a little dog sitting on the bonnet of one of them, which may be the inspiration for the 15th Auxiliary Omnibus Coy unit badge. Three further photographs from the Royal Logistic Corps Museum are much clearer and confirm that the vehicles have Locomobile chassis. The company then moved to Saint-Valery-sur-Somme to join the Auxiliary (Omnibus) Park. In a period of three days 42 vehicles needed repairs, and the Company had to be made up to strength with 38 Daimler lorries and four charabancs. In May 1919 the Company was disbanded.

16th Auxiliary Omnibus Company

The Royal Marine Transport Company and their Daimler buses was taken over as the Army Service Corps' 16th Auxiliary Omnibus Company in October 1915 and attached to the Fourth Army, based at St. Omer. The Coy only had 46 buses left after the retreat from Antwerp, and by 5 November 1915 received as replacements 15 Daimler buses and 21 Locomobile charabancs. After transferring 7 Daimler buses, 8 Daimler lorries and 1 LGOC lorry to 358 Coy. MT ASC, the 16th was left with 75 buses (of which 21 were charabancs), 3 motor cars, 3 lorries and 6 motorcycles - the correct establishment for an omnibus

company.[18] Lance Corporal F Gower joined them in September 1915 when replacement drivers were needed to make up for the Royal Marine drivers who had elected not to transfer to the Army. He had been a Daimler bus driver in Hastings, Sussex, before the war and was serving with the 20th Division Ammunition Column at St.Omer. He describes how the company was divided into four sections with 25 vehicles in each section. When the 16th moved to Saint-Valery-sur-Somme in February 1917 he was in the section of 25 buses which was attached to the Fifth Army. In March 1919 the company was waiting at Wissant, northern France, to be disbanded. During this period it sent 35 drivers for temporary duty in England. The War Diary records that on 23 April 1919 the '16th Auxiliary Bus Coy ceases to exist'.

18th Auxiliary Omnibus Company

The 588 Coy MT ASC was formed in September 1915, at Grove Park and went to France on 19 February 1916, with 23 vehicles on the *SS Glendevon* and 46 vehicles on the *SS Arvonian*. On arrival in France they were attached to the Fourth Army, redesignated as the 18th Auxiliary Omnibus Company in February 1916. on 1 March 1917, 25 charabancs were transferred to the 50th Auxiliary Omnibus Company for the Fourth Army bus section. The Coy moved to the Auxiliary (Omnibus) Park MT at Saint-Valery-sur-Somme in the same month, under the command of Captain A G Sauley.[19] The Company was disbanded on 14 May 1919.

Left
Troops embussing at the Western Front, 1915.
1998/39220

Above
B-type body on American
Locomobile truck chassis.
Michael Young collection

1   Ken Blacker. 'Bus Ride to Death', in *Old Motor Magazine*, volume 5, number 4 (January 1967), pp 151-154.

2   Private Edward James Darby M1/6948, 46 Coy ASC-MT, 2nd Cavalry Division, BEF. *'How to become a Soldier' in one month*. [Manuscript.] London Transport Museum Library reference B061, Box 1, 0418/2000.

3   Records at Imperial War Museum of Driver D V Lewis, 1st Auxiliary Omnibus Coy, Army Service Corps.

4   Records at Imperial War Museum of Driver D V Lewis, 1st Auxiliary Omnibus Coy, Army Service Corps.

5   Jess Dixon [ed.]. *Little Grey Partridge, The Diary of Ishobel Ross*. Aberdeen: Aberdeen University Press, 1988.

6   *Dad's War* (The diary of Private D R Trenbath). See http://freepages.genealogy.rootsweb. ancestry.com/~sheilaweston/trenbath/ dadswar.htm [accessed 28 May 2014].

7   Harold Ashton. 'Coming of the Conductorette', *War Illustrated*, 21 July 1917

8   Mark Lloyd, *The London Scottish in the Great War*. London: Leo Cooper, 2001.

9   Lieutenant Colonel J H Lindsay. *The London Scottish in the Great War*. Place: (Regimental HQ), 1925.

10 Record by Driver D. V. Lewis, Imperial War Museum.

11 Letter from Lance Corporal F Gower, Imperial War Museum.

12 War Diary, 2nd Auxiliary Omnibus Coy, National Archives, Kew, WO 95/148.

13 War Diary, Auxiliary Omnibus Park, National Archives, Kew, WO 95/145, 95/146, 95/147.

14 Private Edward James Darby M1/6948, 46 Coy ASC-MT, 2nd Cavalry Division, BEF. *'How to become a Soldier' in one month*. [Manuscript.] London Transport Museum Library reference B061, Box 1, 0418/2000.

15 Ernest Shephard [eds. Bruce Rossor with Richard Holmes]. *A Sergeant-Major's War: from Hill 60 to the Somme*. Marlborough: The Crowood Press in association with Anthony Bird, 1987.

16 War Diary – 51st Auxiliary Omnibus Coy. National Archives reference WO 95/149.

17 War Diary – 15th Auxiliary Omnibus Coy. National Archives reference WO 95/149.

18 War Diary – 16th Auxiliary Omnibus Coy. National Archives reference WO 95/149

19 War Diary – 18th Auxiliary Omnibus Coy. National Archives reference WO 95/149.

The world wasn't made in a day;
And Eve didn't ride on a 'bus,
But most of the world's in a sandbag
And the rest of it's plastered on us.

The Wipers Times, No 1,
Vol 1 Saturday 12th February, 1916

The Headquarters of the Auxiliary (Omnibus) Park MT at Saint-Valery-sur-Somme, Picardie, was formed in December 1916 with Lieutenant Colonel G L H Howell appointed as commanding officer. Driver Lewis of the 1st Auxiliary Omnibus Company wrote that he believed the Auxiliary (Omnibus) Park MT had been formed at the special instigation of General Haig because of his experiences at the Battle of Loos in September 1915. At Loos, the Germans had not been expecting an attack, and when the 47th (London Territorials) and the 15th (Scottish) divisions breached the second German line, there were no reserves immediately available to exploit the success. This was because the British Commander -in-Chief Sir John French, had kept the reserves - the 21st and 24th Divisions - under his own command 16 miles back from the front-line at Noeux-les-Mines (6 kilometres south of Bethune). By the time they had been released and marched up to the line they were exhausted and too late to be of any use, and the attack failed. French was relieved of his post and Haig took over as Commander-in-Chief. Lewis says that his fellow drivers called the 1st Auxiliary Omnibus Company 'Haig's Company' and felt that they had been chosen specially by him.

It is more likely, however, that the reorganisation took place after the visit by Sir Eric Geddes, deputy director general of Munitions Supply, to study transport in France. Geddes had wide experience of railway operation and had used several managers from the Great Eastern Railway to support him in his work. He concluded about all the Army transport in France and Belgium: 'The organisation was bad; responsibility was divided, and no-one realised the need for transportation until they broke the machine which was never designed to stand the strain... They had no statistics, they were short of material; short of foresight; short of programmes; short of labour and imagination'.

On investigation of the massed fleet of troop carrying vehicles in his charge at the Auxiliary (Omnibus) Park MT, Lieutenant Colonel Howell found that the buses of the Auxiliary Omnibus Coys had been very heavily used. One Army had even requested double the number of drivers so the buses could be worked non-stop, day and night. The vehicles would need a major overhaul at the new base at Saint-Valery-sur-Somme before they could be fully operational.

Driver Mahoney of 1st Auxiliary Omnibus Coy describes how he drove from Godewaersvelde to Saint-Valery-sur-Somme in February 1917 in the worst winter of the war: 80% of the buses of the Company were out of action, mostly due to radiator damage caused by freezing. Even the remaining buses were not in good condition.[1]

Mahoney's own vehicle, which had just been thoroughly overhauled, had to be left behind. He sat on the front mudguard of another bus, stuffing snow into the radiator to cool the engine. Gallons of extra water were carried to replace fluid leaking steadily from the split radiator tubes.

Above
Buses at Saint-Valery-sur-Somme, 1917. Drivers insulated their engines with blankets and straw, but radiators routinely froze overnight.
2014/3839

Opposite
Battle-scarred B-types and exhausted troops, at Saint-Valery-sur-Somme.
1998/36606

Above
Repairs to a B-type lorry at the Auxiliary Omnibus Park.
1998/84868

Despite this they had to stop every six or seven miles to top up. They could only cover 50 miles a day, and at night when they stopped, Mahoney had to walk up to the head of the convoy, one and a half miles away, to get food, which was then too cold to enjoy. He and his mate preferred to eat bread and cheese and spend the time saved in extra sleep. At one stop they saw ducks frozen into the ice of a pond and several drivers fell through the ice when they tried to capture them.[2]

On arriving at Saint-Valery-sur-Somme on 16 February 1917 they were issued with picks and shovels, and had to spend two hours making a new road on which to park their vehicles. They could then have a hot meal and get some 'sleep, glorious sleep.'[3] Mahoney was lucky enough to be given a commission in the Royal Flying Corps and transferred in March 1917. Driver Lewis says the drivers never removed their clothes. Even the sea froze and the water cans carried on the sides of the buses froze solid and bulged.

The work of the overhaul was severely handicapped, both by the weather and by the very large number of men on the sick list who were off duty for long periods. It was discovered that the 2nd and 16th Auxiliary Omnibus Coys were almost completely inoperative and required a major overhaul for every vehicle. The 15th and 18th Companies needed almost as much attention.

339 Coy ASC/ 7 GHQ Ammunition Park became 51st Auxiliary Omnibus Coy in February 1917. This involved a major reorganisation: 213 men, drivers, and artificers together with two workshop lorries, two store lorries and five other lorries were acquired from the 1st, 3rd and 8th GHQ Ammunition Parks. The six Royal Artillery officers and 473 men who dealt specifically with the storage, carriage and delivery of ammunition were transferred to the 8th GHQ Ammunition Park.

3rd Auxiliary Omnibus Company /4 GHQ Ammunition Park became 50th (Headquarters) Auxiliary Omnibus Coy. Their War Diary reveals that they set off on 17 December 1916 with three of their lorries having to be towed. Having arrived at Saint-Valery-sur-Somme the commanding officer was at once sent off to Calais to expedite the preparation of timber for the conversions and transport it back to Saint-Valery. Once the first fifteen lorries had been converted, convoy practice began on 2 January 1917. By transferring out a large number of Maudslay and British Berna lorries in exchange for Swiss Berna lorries they managed by 28 January 1917 to get a homogenous group of 124 Swiss Berna lorry-buses and the official transfer was made to become 50th Auxiliary Omnibus Coy. The convoy drill was by then greatly improved.

Many buses had their passenger bodies removed and replaced with fully open charabanc bodies. Driver Lewis described the conversion of his Swiss Berna lorry to a troop carrier by having planed pine plank seats fitted longways, down each side of his lorry by means of iron brackets, so that they could be quickly removed to enable the vehicle to be used for carrying materials. Lewis remarked that the seats were too narrow to sleep on, as every time he turned over he fell off the seat.[4] It was not only the vehicles which were in short supply. On 12 April 1917, 15 new charabancs arrived, but owing to the shortage of trained men, each had only one driver.

After the reorganisation was completed, the Auxiliary (Omnibus) Park MT consisted of a total of 650 vehicles manned by 1,800 men.[5] (This did not include the independent Army bus sections of 25 buses or charabancs each.) The Park could carry the entire infantry and dismounted engineers of a Division in one move. The strength of the Park was 324 buses, each with a capacity of 25 men, and 271 troop carrier lorries, each carrying 20 men, giving a total capacity of 13,520 men

2nd and 18th Coys were the first to leave Saint-Valery-sur-Somme to go to the Third Army at Frévent in time for the Battle of Arras. By 13 March 1917 the reorganisation was almost completed and 50th, 15th and 51st Coys left Saint-Valery-sur-Somme for Amiens. A complex system of routes, embussing and debussing points had to be set up so that movements could be made quickly and smoothly. The development of this organisation took some time and practice. The 10th Battalion of the Essex Regiment were involved in experiments in bus movements in March 1917. The 53rd Brigade (of which the 10th Essex were part) and the 54th Brigade, totalling together 5,000 men, were moved by a tremendous column of buses through Amiens after waiting three hours at their pick-up point. Their historian says: 'A long day but a useful one, for we never found authority getting quite such a mass of troops together at one embussing point again; nor did we ever wait quite so long for the move to begin, or march so far after debussing'.[5]

Once they had been rehearsed, the bus columns could be ready to move within an hour of the order being given. It usually took only thirty minutes to embus a Division and the record for a Brigade was four and a half minutes. The seven companies of the Auxiliary (Omnibus) Park were located at intervals on the main road through Amiens-Doullens-St. Pol to Ypres. A combined traffic map for the whole front was made showing Army areas, direction of traffic on all roads and embussing and debussing points, which were also labelled on the ground. Such a huge column of vehicles was a formidable sight and there were many complaints made from other units who had been held up by this enormous convoy. Lieutenant Colonel Howell wrote a report in reply to these complaints in which he argued that the column of buses should be treated just like a railway train on a track and no other columns should expect to be able to cross while it was passing.

The majority of movements were made at night without lights and great skill was needed from the drivers to keep up with the vehicles in front. The column was subdivided into smaller sections to leave room for overtaking light vehicles. It was easy for the lead driver in each section to miss the fact that the column had turned and, if he continued on, it might take hours to get the following column stopped and turned round to find the correct route. Two buses were lost by collisions with trains at level crossings at night, when neither vehicle nor train were showing lights.

The Auxiliary (Omnibus) Park MT had a big part to play in the sudden return to mobile warfare that occurred after the big German offensive in March 1918. For example, on 10 April, 2nd and 50th Auxiliary Omnibus Coys moved one Brigade of the 29th Division from Provens. It was found impossible to reach their destination as the enemy was already in possession. The troops were debussed at 03.00 and the vehicles had to reverse, in the dark, back down the road to Bailleul. They were shelled and fired upon by aeroplanes, losing two men killed and six wounded.

Lance Corporal Gower had been sent from 16th Auxiliary Omnibus Coy to be one of the drivers of the 25 vehicles of the 5th Army Bus Section in January 1917, and thought it was a fairly cushy number as there was no convoy work. In February 1918, his bus and two others were attached to the 5th Army Training School at Toutencourt to be used for transporting officers to and from their units for various courses. The Germans broke through the British line on 21 March 1918 and two days later, whilst driving his bus full of officers back from a course, Gower found the road increasingly full of transport going the other way. When he finally found a staff officer to tell him what was going on, he was advised to return to the School. There the entire staff and every available man were loaded onto the three buses and two lorries of the

Opposite
The orders for the 11th Battalion, Royal Fusiliers (54th Brigade) state that packs were to be worn slung so they could easily be removed before climbing on the buses.
1998/36575

DERRIÈRE LA LIGNE DE BATAILLE : LES CONVOIS   DE T. M. (Transport de Matériel) ET T. P. (Transport de Personnel).

Dessin d'après nature de GEORGES SCOTT.

Left
No photographs
of nocturnal bus
movement survive,
but this illustration
of a French army
convoy gives an
idea of the scale of
operations.
2013/11800

transport section, and told they were part of 'Carey's Force'.[6] They were driven to Villers-Brettoneux and told to dig a line of reserve trenches and hold them for four days when they could expect to be relieved by regular troops. In the event they had to man them for a week, when their trenches were taken over by Australian forces. Rather gladly they were able to retreat slowly, with their heavily overloaded buses, until they reached Sailly-le-Sec, where after being lost to their parent unit for six weeks, they were reclaimed.

Many examples can be quoted of the work of the buses during these chaotic weeks. For example, the 4th and 3rd Dismounted Brigades were sent on buses on 21 March 1918 to fill gaps in the line of the 18th Division. Bandsman L. Osborne of the 11th East Yorkshires was hurriedly woken at 3am to be marched forward.[7] The East Yorkshires were then put on one of a row of buses, where his battalion sat for an hour while conflicting orders arrived at Battalion HQ, until they were finally moved off, towards shelling that was so severe that he thought the war was just commencing. All these hurried troop movements meant that often the horse-drawn transport and artillery was left far behind. On 23 March, the 4th Guard's Brigade of the 31st Division were embussed to reinforce the 34th Division. The divisional artillery had a long march and arrived several hours later. On 24 March, the 42nd Division (under Major General Arthur Solly Flood) was brought up in buses without artillery, engineers or transport to relieve the 40th Division. The extent of the chaos on the roads can be imagined when one reads the report of the Prince of Wales Own Civil Service Rifles (15th Battalion, London Regiment) on 9 April 1918.[8] They had been bussed back from the line and halted on the road by a village, where a draft of 600 replacements for their battalion had been waiting all day. As soon as it was dark the draft were told to march to their billets in the next village, three and a half miles away. They arrived an hour before the buses.

By the end of the German attack the Auxiliary (Omnibus) Park MT had worked incredibly hard, carrying British, Canadian, Australian and French troops, and transporting nearly a quarter of a million men over 855,000 miles. In six weeks, sufficient repairs were made that each bus visited the workshops four times. In all this troop transport work, two men were killed and six wounded.[9]

The British Commander-in-Chief, Field Marshal Sir Douglas Haig, wrote to Lieutenant Colonel Howell on 6 May 1918 expressing his great appreciation of the services that they had rendered since 21 March stating: 'The details of the work they have accomplished, in circumstance of particular hardship and difficulty have been brought to my notice and constitute a record of which every officer and man may well be proud. They may rest assured that in meeting the heavy demands recently made upon them, through long hours of continual

duty both on the road and in the workshops, they have greatly assisted the operation of our troops and have contributed in no small degree to the frustration of the enemy's plans. I thank them for the work they have done and count with confidence upon the same loyal service and devotion in the future'.[10] Twenty one NCOs and men of the Auxiliary (Omnibus) Park MT were awarded the Military Medal for their part in the actions during this period.[11] The list shows exactly three members from each of the seven Auxiliary Omnibus Coys.[12]

The greatest day for the Auxiliary (Omnibus) Park came in August 1918 with preparations for the Battle of Amiens. Sir Douglas Haig had gathered together a large force of tanks, artillery, infantry, and aircraft to make a major assault on the German lines in front of the city of Amiens. Under conditions of great secrecy, large numbers of troops had to be moved forward and then hidden from enemy observation. On 2 August, for example, 400 men of the Tank Corps and 360 machine-gunners were moved. On 8 August, all the Park, including 1st, 2nd, 15th, 16th, 18th, 51st and part of 50th Auxiliary Omnibus Coys, was concentrated in Brigade groups at Amiens ready to move troops forward. An advance Auxiliary (Omnibus) Park MT headquarters was set up in Amiens under the direction of Captain A G Sauley, commanding officer of the 18th Auxiliary Omnibus Coy. The Canadian Army, which was to spearhead the assault, was only moved up from Arras to the start line in front of Amiens, on the day before the attack. At the same time a few Canadian radio operators behind the Ypres front kept up a busy traffic in dummy messages to convince the Germans that the Canadians had not been moved. All movements had to be made at night, without lights, to conceal them from German aerial observation. This huge task, involving long hours of night driving and long days of repair and maintenance work, was marked by the Auxiliary (Omnibus) Park MT being 'Mentioned in Despatches', the only Army Service Corps

unit to be so honoured during the War. Some drivers had worked 60 hours continuously, without sleep. In September 1918 the Auxiliary (Omnibus) Park MT carried 200,479 men and travelled 642,098 miles.

On 4 May 1919, Major A W Mallinson MC went to Cologne to take command of 1st and 51st Auxiliary Omnibus Coys, which were renamed the Auxiliary Company (MT), Army of the Rhine. With this redeployment the Auxiliary (Omnibus) Park ceased to exist. Final disbandment of the last London buses that had gone to the War took place in January 1920.

Above
A long convoy of buses waits for orders at Cassel, in August 1917. The unit sign of the 1st Auxiliary Omnibus Coy can just be seen on the rear upper deck panel of the third bus from the left.
1998/40302

1   William Mahoney. *War Diary 1915-16*, University of Leeds, Liddle Collection.

2   William Mahoney. *War Diary 1915-16*, University of Leeds, Liddle Collection.

3   William Mahoney. *War Diary 1915-16*, University of Leeds, Liddle Collection.

4   Colonel R Beardon. *The Royal Army Service Corps*, Cambridge: Cambridge University Press, 1931.

5   Danks & Chell. *With the 10th Essex In France*, n.p.: Burt and Son, 1921.

6   'Carey's Force', was an emergency fighting group formed under the command of British Brigadier General George Carey in late March 1918 to defend a gap in the British line near Amiens. It was comprised mainly of Royal Engineers alongside American and Canadian troops. (Source: Colonel G W L Nicholson, CD, Army Historical Section. Official History of the Canadian Army in the First World War - Canadian Expeditionary Force, 1914-1919, Ottawa, Canada: Roger Duhamel FRSC, Queen's Printer and Controller of Stationery, 1962. [available at: http://www.cmp.cpm forces.gc.ca/dhh-dhp/his/docs/CEF_e.pdf, accessed 28 May 2014].

7   B S Barnes. *This Righteous War*, Huddersfield: Richard Netherwod Ltd, 1990.

8   *The History of the Prince of Wales Own Civil Service Rifles*. n.p.: Wyman and Sons, 1921.

9   In a report for April 1918, dated 5 May 1918, Lieutenant Colonel G L H Howell, commanding Officer of the Auxiliary (Omnibus) Park MT, stated that the total of 211,263 troops had been moved, with 349 buses and 311 lorries achieving a total mileage of 855,638. See file WO 95/149, National Archives, Kew, Surrey.

10 Douglas Haig, Field Marshal, Commanding-in-Chief, British Armies in France, to Officer Commanding, Auxiliary (Omnibus) Park MT, 6 May 1918. See file WO 95/149, National Archives, Kew, Surrey.

11 *War Diary – Auxiliary (Omnibus) Park*, The National Archives, Kew, references WO 95/145, 95.146, 95/147.

12 A full list of the men's names, ranks, regimental numbers, and the Auxiliary Bus Company to which they were attached is given in: Michael Young. *Army Service Corps 1902-1918*. London: Pen & Sword Books (Leo Cooper), 2000, p125.

We were unprepared,
We were most unwise;
We have been like that
For centuries –
But we've taught ourselves a thing or two,
And we're muddling through.

July 1, 1916 T W H Crosland (1862–1924)

BUSES CONVERTED FOR OTHER WAR USES

Buses were adapted to suit a number of different purposes. These included cavalry wireless vehicles, mobile workshops, store lorries, charabancs, general lorries, field kitchens, searchlight lorries, mobile pigeon lofts, water tankers, mobile bath units, buses to transport military bands, and ambulances.

Cavalry wireless buses

Some buses were converted to cavalry wireless vehicles as they could keep up with the fast moving horsed columns. (Thomas Clarkson had hired one of his single-decker steam buses to Marconi in Chelmsford for an experimental mobile wireless station in 1908.) From the outside the cavalry wireless buses were indistinguishable from the ordinary buses.

One such bus of the 1st Cavalry Division was stripped down completely after the war for an engineer's report. Remember that this was a vehicle which had done four years hard war service with no workshop repair:

'The manner in which vehicles of this type withstood the arduous conditions of service was good.... The few defects which were disclosed (in the frame) appear to be due to twist, caused no doubt, by the extremely rough usages to which the lorries were put.... In the particular chassis under consideration, four new cross members were fitted and defective rivets were replaced. The frame was then quite serviceable... but wear had take place in the swivel pin holes, largely due to neglect.... Both front leaf springs showed cracks and some leaves were broken.... Several of the front wheel spokes were found to be cracked... for the front wheel bearings..... considerable wear was evident.... Probably due to the fact that the original bushes had been used for a longer period than would have been the case if an ample supply of spares had been available.... The condition of the steering connections was good.... Between the clutch

and the gear box is fitted a length of shaft with a universal joint at each end.... Those at the front were in poor condition, there being several broken balls'.[1]
None of these fairly minor defects had kept the vehicle off the road for a single day in four and a half years.

Mobile workshops

At the beginning of the war each mobile workshop had been built on a trailer, which was towed behind a standard lorry, but in the retreat from Mons they had been found to be too slow and clumsy, and many had been abandoned to the Germans. The workshops were then mounted on lorry chassis.

The most detailed description of the workshop conversions is given by Captain A M Beatson, writing about the vehicles of the Workshop Section in the Supply Column of the Indian Cavalry Division.[4] Half of the Indian Cavalry Supply Column was made up of B-type lorries and none of them needed any base workshop

Above
As a protest at the slowness of demobilisation, one crew sent home a picture from Cologne in 1919 of their cavalry wireless bus, which had served with the 1st Cavalry Division since 1914.
2014/3837

Opposite
M E T Daimler bus bodies in 1919. The bodies were removed from their chassis when converted for use as lorries during the war.
1998/39278

attention during the entire war. This Column had four mobile workshop lorries and four store lorries, both either Daimlers, with 40 HP Silent Knight engines, or Leylands. Each lorry had a portable forge, a six-inch lathe, a wet tool grinder, a pillar drill and foundry equipment. Initially these fittings were powered by an auxiliary petrol engine, but later they were adapted so that the vehicle's own engine drove a generator, creating space for more equipment. (The 3rd Auxiliary Omnibus Coy. used their workshop lorry's generator to power the projector for their cinema.) The lower sides of mobile workshops could be let down on props to provide more working space when the vehicle was stationary, and the upper halves of each side raised provided shelter from rain or sun. Workshop personnel consisted of fitters, turners, blacksmiths, electricians and carpenters.

Store lorries

Store lorries were used by a wide range of army units, mounted on B-types as well as older bus chassis such as Milnes-Daimler and Straker-Squire.

Charabancs

A crude charabanc type of body was fitted to 271 bus and lorry chassis of B-type, Daimler or other make, to create troop carriers. The war diaries of the Auxiliary Omnibus Coys mention Daimler, Swiss and British Berna, Locomobile, Peerless and Maudslay lorries. The interior of these vehicles, recorded on movie film from the Imperial War Museum, shows bench-like wooden seats mounted across the body of the lorry-buses. They were recorded being used for carrying walking wounded and for normal troop transport.

Searchlight lorries

Tilling-Stevens Petro-Electric buses were converted to searchlight lorries. These buses had a petrol engine which drove a generator which then charged batteries.

The power from these was used to drive separate electric motors attached to each wheel. The system was designed to do away with the need for a gearbox and so give a much smoother ride. The batteries were used in the searchlight lorries to power searchlights mounted on the rear platform. The power was also strong enough to be used for electric arc welding. 113 of these vehicles served in Britain and 74 in France.

Mobile pigeon lofts

One of the biggest problems of trench warfare in the First World War was lack of communication. Once troops had gone over the top towards the enemy lines they were lost to the commanding generals. Land telephone lines were easily damaged by enemy artillery fire and could not be laid quickly enough during an advance to be of any practical use. The first 'mobile' trench wireless set needed two men to carry it – and three more to carry the batteries! Life expectancy of the operators once they had stuck a big aerial up in the air was extremely short.

One answer to this problem of communications was the use of carrier pigeons. At the beginning of the war the British Army had no carrier pigeons, although both the French and Belgian armies had an organized service. The commander of the Belgian pigeon service, Commandant Denuit, had tearfully to destroy all his birds and equipment just before the Germans captured Antwerp, setting the lofts of the Grand Colombier on fire with 2,500 birds inside them. The first British birds were fifteen pigeons handed over by the French Army on 11 September 1914. From this small beginning, Captain, later Major Alec Whaley MC. of the Intelligence Corps - a pigeon fancier who had been appointed as Staff Officer, (Pigeons) - began to build up a carrier pigeon service. After transfer to the new Signal Corps in June 1915 he finally created a service with 24,000 birds, 380 expert pigeon handlers and 90,000 men from front-line units

Above
Leyland lorry converted
to mobile workshop.
1990/84030

trained as 'fliers', many by Captain Whaley himself.[3] The pigeon handlers and the birds themselves were selected in England by Lieutenant Colonel A Osman, editor of The Racing Pigeon in civilian life, who was obviously in the ideal position to know the best 'pigeoneers' and the best pigeons. In this he was assisted by the fact that, as corn for pigeon feed was rationed and reserved for those who bred pigeons for the armed forces, anyone who wished to keep a nucleus of breeding birds though the war had to provide birds for military service.[4]

Both horse-drawn pigeon lofts and motor-buses converted to pigeon lofts were used. Captain Whaley first obtained permission to convert motor omnibuses after visiting Advanced Army headquarters at St. Omer on 26 February 1916. Double-decker buses were converted by roofing in the upper deck and adding chicken wire cages as pigeon coops on either side of the upper decks. These coops could be folded down for travelling. The lower deck was used as a feed store and office. Each bus had an expert pigeon fancier NCO and a Royal Engineer (Signals) private 'fatigue man' and held 60 birds. (The horse-drawn lofts held 75 birds.) Six converted buses or 'Motor Mobile Lofts' were used. Six more were ordered in 1917.

The first pigeons from a Motor Mobile Loft gave service when ten birds from No 5 Motor Mobile Loft were sent to the trenches on 16 August 1916. The Fifth Army in March 1918 had 4 Motor Mobile Lofts. Photographs of these bus pigeon lofts show a great deal of variation in details of construction and colour schemes. An early colour scheme was khaki with a broad white horizontal band, chosen so the pigeons could see it easily. The pigeons certainly found this useful in finding their lofts but so did enemy reconnaissance planes: No. 3 Motor Mobile Loft was bombed on 20 February 1917 but no pigeons were killed. Later schemes therefore included full camouflage with added netting. I have found only one written description of a Mobile Motor Loft outside of the War Diary of the Pigeon Service. Captain Edward Vaughan says in his diary of 14 March 1917, written at Herbécourt: 'a motor bus which had been converted into a pigeon loft around which the pigeons were fluttering and cooing'.[5] This vehicle was also inspected by Major Whaley on March 22nd: 'Visited No 3 Motor Mobile Loft at Herbécourt'.

Lofts were positioned some way behind the line, within four hundred yards or so of Corps Headquarters and connected to it by telephone. Mobile pigeon lofts could not move very often as each relocation required extensive retraining of the birds to ensure they returned. Pigeons were sent forward by bicycle, motor-cycle or car to intermediate 'filling points'. From the 'filling points' birds would be collected by 'fliers' sent back from frontline units. Usually, two men were sent in case one was killed or wounded on the way.

They picked up four pigeons in two baskets and had strict instructions on handling the birds. Putting male and female pigeons in the same basket was forbidden, male birds having a blue mark and female birds a red one. They were not allowed to feed them for the first 24 hours but they were allowed to provide water. Even if they were not needed the birds had to be released after 48 hours, far enough away from the front-line so that they did not reveal the position of the unit headquarters to the enemy. New birds had then to be fetched. Messages were written on forms printed on very fine tracing paper, which could be folded very small and put into a little aluminium cylinder attached to the bird's leg. When released they flew back to Corps headquarters, from where the message could be telephoned to Division and then on to Brigade Headquarters, where the information was most often needed.

Opposite
Supplies are unloaded from a train onto B-type lorries, as troop buses pass in the background.
2014/845

Above
First generation
pigeon loft B-type,
1916.
1999/20005

In good weather this process took only an average of 30 minutes. In 1917 lofts were sent forward to Division which cut this time to 25 minutes. Pigeon messages were always given priority, except perhaps for the one told about by Lieutenant Bernard Montgomery (later to become Field Marshal Sir Bernard Law Montgomery, 1st Viscount Montgomery of Alamein), which was said to have been: 'I am fed up carrying this bloody pigeon'.

Pigeons could only be used one way. They were grounded at night or by fog and smoke. They were, however, much faster than the only alternative which was men 'runners' and when one realizes that during attacks, the average casualty rate for 'runners' was about 50%, whereas 90% of pigeons got though (and as each message was usually duplicated and sent by two pigeons very few messages were lost), it can be seen that pigeons saved many lives.

During the retreat that resulted from the German offensive in March 1918 the Motor Mobile Pigeon Lofts did not prove as movable as had been hoped. With the chaos on the roads making withdrawal difficult, 40 horse-drawn and Motor Mobile Lofts were lost to the enemy. Most had been destroyed by fire after the birds had been released, so no mobile loft was captured complete with pigeons. The Fifth Army managed to salvage 3 Motor Mobile Lofts on 27 March 1918. The French Army fared even worse and lost almost all their fixed and mobile lofts. The last recorded use of the Motor Mobile Pigeon Lofts was on 31 January 1919 when Major Whaley saw Nos. 2 and 6 Motor Mobile Lofts at Morville in Belgium on the road to Namur. No. 6 had been damaged because its driver had carelessly driven under a low bridge.

Water tankers

Water Tanker Companies carried drinking water to the front line in various water tanks fitted on the backs of lorries. These were usually Garfords but if a vehicle broke down the water tank was transferred to any available chassis. There is a photo of a 500 gallon water tank on a B-type chassis belong to No 4 Water Tank Company.

Mobile bath unit

One Daimler chassis was used by a unit of female volunteers, the First Aid Nursing Yeomanry (FANY) in the Calais area as a Brown-Hughes & Strachan Motor-Bath, a name shortened by them to 'James'. Fitted with a boiler heated by two furnaces, a water tank and a pump, there was a folding canvas annexe on each side each housing six collapsible canvas baths. It was paid for by two ladies, who both later commanded the FANY: Marian and Hope Gamwell. After providing baths for 600 men in two days it was so bogged down in mud that it had to be towed out by horses.[7] Four Royal Army Medical Corps doctors came to inspect the mobile bath unit on one occasion and one of them, Colonel Fell, got into one of the empty collapsible baths, fully dressed of course, to test it for size. He got stuck and could only be released by the application of considerable force.[8] (The heating unit for these mobile baths was designed by our old friend, Thomas Clarkson. He had been looking for even cheaper fuel and had designed a self-stoking boiler which fed coke automatically to a flash boiler to provide steam for a lorry. The unit proved ideal for providing large quantities of hot water quickly from a relatively small unit and his boilers, fuelled both by coke and oil were used widely. He demonstrated one of these units to King George and Queen Mary at Buckingham Palace.)

Buses to transport military bands

On 26 August 1915 the 16th Auxiliary Omnibus Coy had to provide two buses to carry the band of the No. 6 London Field Ambulance to Arques from Marles-les-Mines. Although the vehicles were not conversions, they are included here as another example of diverse

use. One bus is recorded as being used to carry the band of the 11th Division to various engagements. Even this easy service was not without its dangers as the bus was bombed, and both the drivers and their dog were wounded. One of the Division's band members had been a commercial artist for a motoring magazine before the war and it is possible to see from his very accurate drawings that this bus was a Daimler.[9] This seems to have been a common task for buses. The 15th Auxiliary Omnibus Coy detailed three buses to carry Lord Derby's band to engagements for several days, and another two buses a month later to carry the Third Army band. Driver Mahoney described how, on Christmas morning 1916, after spending three days plucking four geese in preparation for his unit's Christmas dinner, there came an 'urgent' call for two buses to go out on a job. His name was one of the four unlucky drivers whose names were drawn out of a hat to go. When he found that the job was to take the First Army band round to give Christmas concerts to the staff he was very upset. His bus began to overheat going up the steep hill at Cassel (the hill the Grand Old Duke of York marched Ten Thousand Men up and down) where the General Headquarters was situated. When he reached the top his radiator was boiling over and he had to replace the broken fan belt with his braces to be able to carry on.

Ambulances

Some buses were used as ambulances. Not many details exist about these vehicles, but 275 B-type chassis were said to have gone overseas for this purpose, of which only 45 returned. Whenever there was heavy fighting it was usual for two buses to be attached to each Casualty Clearing Station to carry walking wounded back to hospitals down the line of communications. The 16th Auxiliary Omnibus Coy first records this on 27 April 1915 when 22 buses that had been sent to convey drafts from Hazebrouck Station to Vlamertinghe were required to

wait just short of the village because it was being heavily shelled. The buses were turned in the road and during the night they returned singly to base as they filled with wounded. H M Tomlinson records, in July 1915, the story of a bus driver, who had been to Antwerp and so must have been in the 16th Auxiliary Omnibus Coy, who evacuated wounded from the first gas attack of the war at Ypres on 29 April:

'You know Poperinghe? Well, my trip was between there and Wipers [Ypres], gen'ally. The stones on the road was enough to make 'er shed nuts and bolts by the pint. But it was a quiet journey, take it all round and after a quiet cup of tea at Wipers I used to roll home to the park. It was easier than the Putney route. Wipers was full of civilians. Shops all open...
'First thing was the gassed soldiers coming through. Their faces were green and blue, and their uniform a funny colour. I didn't know what was the matter with 'em, and that put the wind up, for I didn't want to look like that. We could hear a gaudy rumpus in the Salient. The civvies were frightened, but they stuck to their homes..... 'After seeing a Zouave crawl by with his tongue hanging out and his face the colour of a mottled cucumber, I said good-bye to the little girl where I was. It was time to see about it. And fact is, I didn't have much time to think about it, what with getting' men out and getting reinforcements in. Trip after trip.

'But I shall never have a night like that one. ...I steered the old 'bus, but it was done by accident. It was certainly touch and go.

'It was like the end of the world. Time for me to 'op it. I backed the old 'bus and turned 'er, and started off – shells in front and behind and overhead, and thinks I, next time you're bound to get caught in this shower. Then I found my officer 'E was smoking a cigarette, and 'e told

Opposite
Mobile pigeon loft based on B-type bus, with full camouflage, 1917-8.
2013/5358

me my job. 'E gave me my cargo and I just 'ad to take 'em out and dump 'em.

'"Where shall I take 'em, sir?"
"Take 'em out of this" says he. "Take 'em anywhere, take 'em anywhere you like, Jones, take 'em to hell, but take 'em away."

'So I loaded up. Wounded Tommies, gassed Arabs, some women and children, and a few genuine cock-eyed loonies from the asylum. The shells chased us out. One biffed us over on to the two rear wheels, but we dropped back on four at the top speed. Several times I bumped over soft things in the road and felt rather sick… Then the old bus jibbed for a bit. Every time a shell burst near us the lunatics screamed and laughed and clapped their hands, and trod on the wounded, but I got her going again. I got 'er to Poperinghe. Two soldiers died on the way, and a lunatic had fallen out somewhere, and a baby was born in the 'bus; and me with no conductor and no midwife.'[10]

On 1 July 1916 the ADMS (Assistant Director of Medical Services) of the 31st Division reported from Bus-les-Artois that 'A motor "bus" sent by DDMS Corps has also been sent and assists in clearing slight cases'. Nine charabancs were provided at Rouen to carry wounded from the railway station to hospital ships. They were rather surprisingly on the strength of the 20th Auxiliary Petrol Company.[11]

Siegfried Sassoon, the poet, wrote about being carried back by motor-bus after being wounded in the shoulder on 16 April 1916: 'in the bus, wedged in among "walking wounded", I was aware that I had talked quite enough. For an hour and a half we bumped and swayed along ruined roads till we came to the Casualty Clearing Station at Warlencourt'.[12] George Coppard was shot in the ankle with a revolver by his mate 'Snowy' by accident on October 17 1916. His wound was dressed and, 'that evening, with other wounded men, I travelled in a very ancient charabanc, past the ruins of Montauban and Longueval, right out of the battle area'.[13]

Single-decker conversions

Photographs show double-decker buses being cut down to single-deckers, One photograph shows such a bus as a vehicle of the 46 Coy. MT. ASC. in use as part of the 2nd Cavalry Divisional troops supply column. Private E Darby of that unit, describes what happened to his bus on 29 October 1914. Soon after the arrival of their company at Rouen they were sent to stretch their legs after being aboard ship for three days: 'It was after returning from our march, that we had a great surprise, for instead of finding orderly lines of busses, we found a party of soldiers, assisted by Frenchmen, were busy demolishing the upper part of the bodies and turning them into open lorries…. My own lorry I christened "Nelson" because it had lost parts of its body and was No 1805'.[14]

1   *Automobile Engineer*, September 1920.

2   A. M. Beatson, *The Motor-Bus In War: being the impressions of an A.S.C. officer during two and a half years at the front.* (London: T. Fisher Unwin, 1918). Beatson was temporary lieutenant in the MT supply column of an Indian Cavalry division. Beatson enlisted early August 1914; he was attached to 93 Company ASC/4th Auxiliary Omnibus Company (MT), which operated box van lorries on former bus chassis.

3   Major General R F H Nalder. *The Royal Corps of Signals: A history of its antecedents and development, circa 1800-1955.* London: Royal Signals Institution, 1958.

4   A H Osman. *Pigeons in the Great War. A complete history of the Carrier Pigeon Service, 1914 to 1918.* London : "Racing Pigeon" Publishing Co., 1929.

5   E C Vaughan [with a foreword by John Terraine]. *Some desperate glory: the diary of a young officer, 1917.* London: Frederick Warne, 1982.

6   *War Diary - The Pigeon Services.* National Archives, Kew, reference WO 95/123, chapter 9.

7   Hugh Popham. *The F.A.N.Y. in peace and war: the story of the First Aid Nursing Yeomanry 1907-2003.* Barnsley: Leo Cooper, 2003.

8   Irene Ward. *F.A.N.Y. Invicta.* London: Hutchinson, 1955.

9   Daphne Jones. *Bullets and bandsmen: the story of a bandsman on the Western Front / written by his daughter.* Downton: Owl Press, 1992.

10 H M Tomlinson. *Waiting for Daylight.* London: Cassell & Co., 1922.

11 Michael Young. *Army Service Corps, 1902-1918.* London: Leo Cooper, 2000.

12 Siegfried Sassoon. *Memoirs of an Infantry Officer. By the author of Memoirs of a Fox-Hunting Man.* London: Faber & Faber, 1930.

13 George Coppard. *With a machine gun to Cambrai: the tale of a young Tommy in Kitchener's army 1914-1918.* London: H M S O, 1969.

14 Private Edward James Darby M1/6948, 46 Coy ASC-MT, 2nd Cavalry Division, BEF. *'How to become a Soldier' in one month.* [Manuscript.] London Transport Museum Library reference B061, Box 1. 0418/2000.

Guerre 1914-15 - ALBERT (Somme) La Place d'Armes
en Août 1914
... d'Automobiles anglaises de Ravitaillement

LE FAMILISTÈRE

Spend our resentment, cannon,
– yea disburse
Our gold in shapes of flame,
our breaths in storm.

On seeing a piece of our heavy
artillery brought into action,
Wilfred Owen (1893–1918)

G. Ledun, 21, rue Saint-Martin, Am...

ARMOURED B-TYPES, ARTILLERY B-TYPES, B-TYPE AND DAIMLER MILITARY LORRIES

CHAPTER EIGHT

Royal Naval Air Service armoured B-type lorries

Commander Samson of the Eastchurch Squadron of the Royal Naval Air Service (RNAS) at Dunkirk had, as part of his transport park, eight B-type LGOC lorries. Two of these lorries, one being B752 (LE9401) which had formerly been the general duty lorry at the London General Omnibus Company's Atholl Street garage, were converted into armoured vehicles by the firm *Forges et Chantiers de France* of Dunkirk. *Forge et Chantiers de France* had already provided improvised armour plate for several armoured cars of the RNAS. They used commercial boiler plate – all that was available at the time – which was only proof against German bullets at ranges greater than 500 yards, so the protection that it provided was more apparent than real. To make the best use of the plate it was sloped at an angle at the sides and back of the lorries and driver's position. To reduce the weight on the chassis, protection for the engine was only partial, consisting of a sloping plate at the front and little side flaps to protect the vulnerable radiator.

Twelve Royal Marines manned the vehicle and could fire their rifles through loopholes in the walls of the rear compartment. They had to climb into this by ladders fixed on either side and there was no overhead protection at all. The armoured lorries had been designed to act as personnel carriers, to provide infantry support for the lighter Talbot, Wolseley and Rolls-Royce armoured cars. They were so heavily loaded with their armour and crew that it was soon found that they could not keep up with the faster armoured cars. They were therefore used as mobile blockhouses to guard important road junctions, such as the crossroads near Samson's headquarters at Hazebrouck. It was found easier to use non-armoured lorries and light trucks in the motorized infantry role. All the different conversions left Samson's men short of heavy lorries, and they would scour the roads around their position looking for broken-down or abandoned lorries

to take back. They also 'won' two lorries from a careless Army Service Corps unit and disguised them by painting RNAS on the sides; they were only prevented from getting a third by the return of the drivers from their dinner.

The two armoured B-type lorries accompanied the 70 Daimler buses to Antwerp to try to support the Royal Naval Division but with the onset of trench warfare they quickly became outmoded and were not used again. The two armoured lorries appear from black and white photos to be painted naval battleship grey, with the letters R N painted on the sides in white.

War Office Pattern B-Type armoured lorries

At the beginning of 1915 the British War Office had arranged for a new type of armoured B-type lorry to be designed and built at Woolwich Arsenal, London. The design was for an armoured personnel carrier. Its armour was largely vertical and it had sliding doors fitted to firing ports for the crew to use their weapons through. The crew position at the front, next to the driver, was fitted with a larger shutter for a machine gun. The armour manufactured by Scottish steelworks William Beardmore & Co. was an improvement on the original RNAS boiler plate, but could still only offer protection against German bullets at ranges above 100 yards.

This project was well under way when it came to the attention of Lord Kitchener, the Minister for War. Knowing that the Royal Naval Air Service were the armoured warfare experts of their day he asked them to send someone to report on the vehicle. Flight Commander T G Hetherington was chosen, as he had had considerable experience with the RNAS armoured vehicles in France and Belgium. Hetherington's adverse comments seem to have put an end to the project. By this time even the lighter armoured cars were of little use and the units were being disbanded.

Opposite
ASC lorries in France, August 1914.
Michael Young collection

1914... Auto blindée du commandant Samson qui détruisit une quantité de uhlans

12me Série

Steel shecter auto of commandant Samson with killed many uhlans

E·L·D

B 752

Above
B752 fitted with armour in Dunkirk, 1914.
William Ward collection

The armoured cars also came to the attention of a German spy, Carl Frederick Müller, who wrote in invisible ink on the back of a seemingly innocent letter dated 20 February 1915 and posted to Holland: 'In Woolwich for ammunition and guns, also armoured car and airships'.[1] The letter was intercepted by the postal censors, because the address in Holland was known to British Intelligence as being one used by the German espionage service. Even after Carl Müller had been executed misleading letters were sent by the British but slowly the Germans came to realize they were being deceived.

It is uncertain how many of these vehicles were built. One reference says of B-type buses that 'at least ten became armoured cars'.[2] Possibly that was the War Office's planned complement. Photographs show the War Office Armoured B-type in two states, the first 'ex-works' with the radiator shutter marked O.H.M.S. and the Ipswich registration number DX 1284, and later versions with the radiator armour removed to improve engine cooling - a common problem with early armoured vehicles. Mudguards were also added to the front wheels. None saw service outside England and they seem to have spent the war on coastal defence duties. One photograph shows a vehicle at Ramsgate, and another shows another vehicle at Bridlington in August 1915. This armoured lorry, with the Hull registration AI 2508, served with the Motor Section of the 2/6th (Territorial) Battalion of the Norfolk Regiment. A further photograph from the Royal Logistic Corps Museum shows two War Office B-type armoured cars together at an unknown site. The vehicles and drivers seem different from any of the other pictures. The colour of the War Office Pattern B-Type Armoured Lorry seems to have been khaki-green with white markings.[3]

The 3-pounder gun lorries

After his return from Antwerp, the inventive Commander Samson of the Royal Naval Air Service at Dunkirk - not content with pioneering strategic bombing, armoured warfare, motorised infantry and armoured personnel carriers - also used one of his B-type lorries B2791, to mount a 3-pounder Vickers quick-firing gun. Most of the design work was done by his brother Felix Samson, in civilian life a solicitor, but now serving with the RNAS as a Lieutenant RNVR (Royal Naval Volunteer Reserve), together with Samson himself and Lieutenant Warner. The gun, mounted on its solid pedestal for ship-board use, was simply bolted onto to the bed of the lorry. The lorry sides were adapted so they could be folded down and fixed horizontally to give a roomier platform for the gun crew in action. A similar gun was also put on what is described as a Mercedes lorry. This may have been an old Milnes-Daimler bus chassis. The actual work was done by the ever resourceful firm of *Forges et Chantiers de France* at Dunkirk, who delivered B2791 on 15 October 1914. Samson himself described the gun-mounting as excellent and said it never gave any trouble whatsoever.[4]

On 16 October the gun lorry was used for the first time, accompanied by an armoured car and a touring car, at Oostnieuwkerke, where the RNAS had been asked to recover the body of an officer killed there the day before. On the way there, some German soldiers had occupied a farm-house. Half a dozen shells from the 3-pounder soon evicted the Germans who were then driven off by the machine gun fire from the armoured car. The three-pounder shells were thought ideal for this job as they were naval issue designed with a delayed action fuse to penetrate armour plate so they went through a brick wall and then exploded inside the building. The lorry was as steady as a rock. The lorry equipment included four tins of petrol, 96 rounds of 3-pounder ammunition, a Lewis gun and the 3-pounder spares box. In addition, the gunner Lieutenant Warner, always insisted on a good supply of food. He never let anyone else fire his gun but paid for this by frequent black eyes from the recoil of the telescopic sight. The driver was called Redmond and the usual crew was Armourer's Mate Hughes, Gunner Platford and Private Edmunds.

The next day, 17 October 1914, together with two armoured cars, they first enfiladed a German trench near Kezelberg causing heavy casualties. They then saw a windmill's sails begin to revolve, a common means of sending signals, and shot a German observer as he tried to climb down the mill's ladder. On 19 October they checked a German attack on the Lifeguards at Moorslede, firing forty shells in co-operation with some horse-artillery guns. The roads were becoming increasingly broken-up by heavy traffic and shelling and on 20 October the lorry broke a spring, which put it out of action for two days until it could be repaired by the Poperinghe blacksmith.

Two days later the lorry went to Zandvoort, but the poor state of the roads meant that it was held up near a cottage by a canal. Here, two German parties tried to cross the canal by two bridges but were shelled. A group of Germans got to within 200 yards and opened a sudden heavy rifle fire. Fortunately the gun shield proved bullet-proof and 3-pounder shells soon suppressed the firing with no British casualties, but there were a lot of bullet marks on the lorry and the accompanying armoured car. On 23 October 1914 at Hollebeke, they shot up some horse-drawn wagons. By now the bad weather had made many roads virtually impassable. On 10 November, at the request of the Belgian army, the gun was sent to Kerkmolenburg where 500 Germans were entrenched in a group of buildings. The Belgian artillery, only having shrapnel rounds, was unable to evict them. As soon as the gun lorry opened fire the German artillery replied. The lorry refused to start and the crew dived into a nearby ditch. After ten minutes they took advantage of a lull in the firing to make a dash for it.

Redmond started the lorry with the first turn of the starting handle and then set off at top speed down the road, dodging the shells and craters. Although the gun lorry had further outings on 14 and 15 November it was becoming obvious that, with the advent of trench warfare, the mobile days of the gun lorry was over. The gun was removed and transferred to an 80-foot launch, although it had fired so many rounds that it was described as being virtually a 'smoothbore'. Samson was ordered back to England with his transport. B2791 survived the war and was reacquired by the LGOC in 1919, refurbished as a bus and served for many years. Its London passengers cannot have suspected what an interesting 37 days it had spent in 1914.

The 13-pounder anti-aircraft gun lorries
The British Army used as some of its earliest anti-aircraft guns (former 13-pounder horse-artillery weapons) mounted on B-type bus chassis (B3885-B3902) in December 1914. The guns were converted for their new role by being fitted on to a simple improvised mount made of steel plate.[5] The sides of the lorry could be folded down to enlarge the fighting platform and the lorry jacked up on blocks to take some of the recoil from the gun when firing. Two kinds of shell could be used, shrapnel and High Explosive (HE). Used at high angle the HE shells proved dangerous, sometimes exploding inside the barrel and bursting the gun. Some of the problem was the inability of the factories, hurriedly turned into munition works, to manufacture shells to the standards required. It took until early 1916 before the problem was solved and the gunners could depend on reliable ammunition. On 9 May 1915 these guns are recorded as being distributed, with 6 in the First Army, 7 in the Second Army and 5 in reserve and at GHQ. Only half of the Divisions in France had an Anti-Aircraft (A-A) section of two guns.

Top left
Daimler with Vickers
anti-aircraft gun.
*Terry Gosling
collection*

Above
LGOC staff building
lorry bus bodies at
North Road, 1914.
1998/36511

Left
Felix Samson's
three-pounder gun
mounted on B2791,
seen at Dunkirk.
The Tank Museum

A bus driver serving with the 10th Anti-Aircraft Section, wrote home with a photograph of two gun lorries in April 1915:

'I got appointed to this Anti-Aircraft Section which consists of a quick-firing gun mounted on a B-Type Lorry, also Daimler ammunition lorries.... The best of it is, I have a kit of tools to fit with, just about suitable to keep a few grass rollers and mangles [sic] in order.... The weather we like best here ourselves is wet, windy and cloudy days, for then we get no planes over, but on a clear day we are kept busy popping away at them. It is an expensive game too; each of our shells is supposed to cost 32/ each, and one day last week we fired 126 rounds. You ought to see the old B. Type buck-jumping when the gun fires, but she sticks it like a brick'.[6] Three months later, in July, however, he wrote home, 'Our poor old 'B. type' has at last given up the ghost under the strain of continual firing; her chassis broke in the middle, and her place has been taken by a "3-tonner" of a different make'.[7]

The War Diary of No. 10 Anti-Aircraft Section for 3 April 1915 records the problems with the B-type chassis: 'Holding down girder on B section gun found to be badly bent. Sent in lorry and hand straightened and a block of wood inserted behind girder on floor of lorry. This will do as a temporary measure but the front girder will have to be replaced by a cranked one or there will be danger of the cardan shaft hitting it on bad roads. I am having these made for both guns'. On 22 April 1915 a further entry states: 'A' gun sent to the 9th A.A. Section at Ypres. This gun brought back to GHQ on damaged LGOC lorry. This is the gun they brought out with them in November from Woolwich to form 9 section'. On 9 August 1915 the writer of the diary records 'A section lorry rapidly disintegrating'.[8]

Although improved guns were produced on stronger lorry chassis, the 13-pounder Anti-Aircraft weapons were kept in service until the end of the war, when some of them were taken off their lorry mounts and returned to the horse artillery. Some of them still remain in service with the King's Troop to fire ceremonial salutes and take part in Troop riding demonstrations.

B-type and Daimler lorries: pre-war production

The B-type chassis had been designed by Frank Searle in 1910 and the Daimler chassis in 1912. Searle had been working to very stringent dimensions to comply with the rigid regulations for buses applied by the London Metropolitan Police Licensing Authority. The result was that the two chassis were virtually identical and bus bodies could readily be transferred between them. The Gearless Company used B-type bodies on Daimler chassis, and during the war the LGOC used Daimler bodies from store on B-type chassis.

When the Underground group took over the MET Company it cancelled part of the order for Daimler buses and made up the number with B-types. To compensate the Daimler company at Coventry for this loss of orders they were given the agency to sell all B-type chassis outside London. Daimlers were unable to complete all their orders for chassis from their own resources and so they sold many Walthamstow-made AEC B-type chassis, with either Daimler or LGOC engines, but all with Daimler radiators as the Daimler 'X-type'.

As we saw earlier, the B-type lorry did not conform to the very detailed requirements of the Subsidy regulations but it was recognized as eligible for Subsidy payments from 1913. These rigid controls had meant that a fault in any one type of Subsidy vehicle tended to occur in all the other different makes; during the war field workshops had long lists of modifications to be made, where possible, to Subsidy vehicles passing through their hands. The B-type however had only one modification suggested.[9]

War-time operation

When buses were called up for service in 1914 those designated for use as lorries were initially fitted with lorry bodies by the LGOC's three coachbuilding works, and sent to the Army Service Corps depot at Grove Park to be allocated to the various units. The earlier vehicles had the same fitted cab that the AEC Walthamstow factory had provided for its own garage lorries, but later versions received a folding canvas hood. None of the lorries had a windscreen as glass was considered too dangerous for military use, so the only protection for the drivers was removable canvas screens.

When heavy repairs were necessary they were often done by mobile workshops, themselves mounted on B-type or Daimler chassis. There were two heavy repair depots at Paris and Rouen for motor transport and the No. 1 Depot at Rouen held all the spare parts for AEC and Daimler vehicles. A special Retrieving Section was set up in 1918 to salvage spare parts from wrecked vehicles and it even collected scrap metal to cast new parts.

The American B-type

In early 1914 the LGOC had planned to replace all of their older types of buses with B-types and wanted 500 chassis from AEC to enable them to do this. The AEC were unable to build such a large order in the time available so they ordered 500 chassis from the United States to be shipped over in parts and assembled in England. The working drawings and specifications were sent across the Atlantic and in the early months of the war the new parts began to arrive. The American parts were then found to be heavier than their British counterparts, so that a chassis built from them resulted in a bus that was too heavy for the London Metropolitan Police regulations. These units, numbered B4715 to B5214, were therefore used for war order lorries and single deck buses (B4869 to B4878) where weight limits were less critical. In April 1916 the AEC was asked to provide 450 chassis for 3-ton lorries for the Russian government. The chassis numbered B4714 to 4864 and were called the Russian Z type. The order was cut to 150 in May and completed by October 1916.

The Russian B-type

Some 250 of the American B-type chassis were built by AEC for the Russian government as 2-ton lorries (B7415-7564). This was the smallest vehicle that AEC ever built. This version, known as the Russian or R-type, had a shortened frame. It had an AEC pattern radiator, a louvered bonnet, high square dashboard, 7-spoked front wheel and 8-spoked rear wheels. The Russian roads were exceptionally bad and it seems that they needed a vehicle which, although it carried a fairly small load, had a reserve of engine power to get it through the muddy and rutted conditions usual in that country. Another batch of 150 vehicles (B7565-7664) was built in 1916-17, but because of the Russian revolution 72 were diverted to the American YMCA.

1   Leonard Sellers. *Shot in the Tower*. London: Leo Cooper, London 1997, p. 53.

2   G J Robbins & J B Atkinson. *The London B-type motor omnibus*. Twickenham: DPR Marketing and Sales The World of Transport, 1991.

3   Some pictures of Fiat 15TER armoured lorries in India have a pattern of armour plating that looks so similar to the War Office Pattern vehicles that it is possible that part of the original order at Woolwich was cancelled and the surplus armour plate was sent to India.

4   Air-Commodore Charles Rumney Samson. *Fights and flights*. London: Benn, 1930.

5   The addition of a spring clip to the breech prevented a round from falling out when loaded with the gun at a high angle. An extra spring recuperator was added above the original one to help return the gun to the firing position more quickly when firing at high elevation. A metal plate was riveted alongside the breech to prevent the gun layer being struck by the recoiling barrel as the gun swung round to follow an aircraft.

6   Letter from Driver A. Phillips, 10th Section, Anti-Aircraft, in *TOT* magazine, No 15, April 1915.

7   Further Letter from Driver A. Phillips, 10th Section, Anti-Aircraft, in *TOT* magazine, No 15, April 1915.

8   Diary of No 10 Anti-Aircraft Section, National Archives, Kew, reference WO 95/4049.

9   To lower the compression ratio of the engine to enable it to cope with poor quality war-time petrol, it was suggested that a steel plate be inserted under the cylinders. The bus companies had been forced to learn in a hard economic school that they had to have tough, reliable vehicles, which could be rapidly and easily repaired. To be fair, the manufacturers of Subsidy lorries had only had one year to iron out problems with their vehicles before the war started, unlike the bus manufacturers who had had more than four years.

Happy the traveller whose eye may range
O'er Lemnos, Samothrace and Helles' strait,
Who smells the sweet thyme-scented breezes. Nay,
How willingly all these I would exchange,
To see the buses throng by Mile End Gate
And smell the fried fish shops down Limehouse way.

Lemnos 1915. Capt. Clement Attlee (1883–1967)

We have already seen how the Royal Navy requisitioned thirty single deck buses in August 1914 for use as ambulances at the naval ports. A large number of buses were used at home for War Service, often as hired vehicles from the Private Hire Department of the LGOC. Some seem to have been used in a less official manner. The *Commercial Motor* for 17 September 1914 has an item headed 'Troops in London': 'Cases have occurred in which military officers have thought fit to commandeer public-service vehicles for moving troops about London when they have not been actually proceeding abroad to active service. Orders have now been given that this must cease immediately. All movements of parties across London must be made by the Underground Railway'.[1]

The LGOC soon lost a lot of buses. All the 272 Daimlers of the MET and Gearless companies had gone to France, either as buses or lorries. Then 300 B-type buses were sent to France in September 1914 and another 300 were requisitioned for military duties in England. These are described as being for London defence duties, air raid work and carrying wounded and convalescent soldiers. The VAD (Volunteer Aid Detachment) of the Prudential Insurance Company had a car and a bus allocated to them in September 1914.[2] These vehicles were kept parked in the courtyard of the Prudential's head office on Holborn, London. A detachment of men volunteered to sleep there in order to be available for any late night calls to carry wounded from the railway stations to hospitals.

The LGOC was hard pressed to find enough buses to maintain its London services, especially with extra demands for new bus services to munition factories, and had to resort to a number of expedients. All its remaining B-type lorries had bus bodies fitted – either single or double deck - and the lorry bodies were transferred to older De Dion-Bouton chassis. Some of the less modern classes of buses, such as the X-type, Straker-Squire and

Above
A Private Hire bus brings wounded soldiers to town for a show at the Palace Theatre, London.
1998/70313

Opposite
Group of wounded soldiers pose with a bus at Millbank Hospital, London.
1998/90001

Left

A group of Belgian refugee children take a Christmas trip on an LGOC bus, 1914.
1998/87137

Bottom left

B804, hit near Liverpool Street during a Zeppelin raid in September 1915.
1998/33334

Bottom right

Postcard of a wreath-laden bus, commemorating the funerals of the LGOC bus crew killed in the Zeppelin raid on 8 September 1915.
1983/191/2

De Dion-Bouton, were also re-licenced for public service in April and May 1915, mostly for War Department work. Fifty L-type Leylands were also used. One photograph shows two M-types carrying Belgian troops in London. They were all wearing medals so probably had been to an investiture. Other photographs show more everyday groups such as Portuguese forestry workers being carried by bus.

The number of buses was also reduced by enemy action. On the evening of 8 September 1915, for example, Kapitan-Leutnant Heinrich Mathy's airship L13 dropped many bombs across London. The author D H Lawrence was below and wrote in a letter the next day: 'Then we saw the Zeppelin above us, just ahead, high up, like a bright golden finger.....Then there were flashes near the ground – and the shaking noise'.[4] Mathy's assistant engineman described the results: 'We dropped the rest of the load over a railway station and had the satisfaction of seeing rails and ties and pieces of depot and two big buses spouting in the air and then dropping back in a mass of wreckage. It was easy to see all this because we had dropped so many incendiaries and there were pools and rivers of fire along all the streets'.[5]

These two buses were B804, just turning from Blomfield Street into Liverpool Street, and B979 at Norton Folgate. The time was just 22.30. Florence Williams, a passenger in bus B979 wrote later: 'I boarded the No.8 bus at Old Ford....Looking up in the sky, I saw the searchlights meet on a Zeppelin. As the bus went on round Norton Folgate, I was very frightened and started to cry.... Something seemed to tell me to get off the bus and I broke away.... There was an explosion and a blinding flash like lightning....I felt myself going down and my fall was broken by a man on the bottom step....He lay in the road with my hat in his hand and was later picked up dead....I just got a glimpse of the conductor still standing at his post on the platform. It turned out I had been peppered with shrapnel.[6] Mr H W Player described how he was a passenger on B804: 'There were eight passengers, and six were killed or died shortly afterwards. I was, of course, knocked unconscious, but have some recollection of being inside a blazing bus and stumbling over someone on the floor. When I came to, I found myself hobbling along the road and I think I remember hearing some more explosions behind me'.[7] A bomb had fallen on the bonnet of the bus. The driver's seat was found on the roof of Liverpool Street Station. Mr. Player spent three months in the London Hospital being treated for six wounds in his thigh.

Zeppelin L13 escaped and flew back to Germany passing over Faulkbourne, in Essex, where it was heard by Ruth Beardwell and recorded in her diary: 'Sept. 8th. Another air raid. Liverpool Street Station damaged. We heard the Zeppelin as it returned'.[8] On 9 September Michael MacDonagh, a reporter for *The Times*, visited the scene: *'I came to the site where a bomb dropped in front of a motor omnibus bound for Liverpool Street Station and blew it to pieces. Twenty people were on board, including the driver and conductor. Nine were killed instantly and eleven seriously injured.*[9] He reported that during this raid 38 people were killed, including two policemen, and 124 injured. Property damage was over £½million. In tracing these histories, it will be noticed that there are discrepancies between accounts, but in view of the awful happenings these are not surprising. Both buses were repaired, fitted with new bodies and returned to service in the same month.

Air raids damaged other buses. Michael MacDonagh reported a Zeppelin raid on Holborn on 14 October: 'The policeman on duty told me that the driver and conductor of a passing omnibus were killed by the explosion and also one of the passengers'. He also

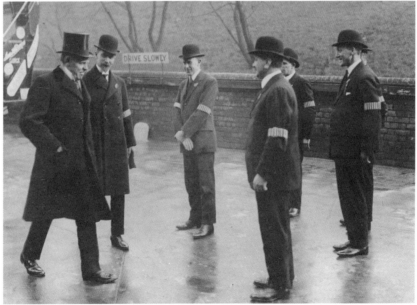

Left
Women mechanics
work on a B-type bus.
1998/84468

Bottom left
Lithograph of
a female bus
conductor, from
Archibald Hartrick's
War Work series,
1918.
1985/3/7

Bottom right
Lord Ashfield
inspects LGOC
Special Constables
at Cricklewood in
March 1916. Their
duties included
supervising queues,
as well as first aid
and salvage work
following air raids.
1998/73841

reported the ending of Mathy when L31 was shot down: 'One body was found in a field some distance from the wreckage. He must have jumped from the burning airship from a considerable height....Life was in him when he was picked up but the spark soon went out....The dead man was Heinrich Mathy'.

By the end of 1915 the supply of new lorries for the War Department had increased sufficiently to meet demand and the LGOC were allowed to buy back from the government 108 B-type buses from the home service batch. They were quickly put back into public service. One of these buses was B340 which is now in the London Transport Museum in Covent Garden, with a replacement post-First World War body.

The British Bus Company, the fleet name for British Automobile Development Limited, had taken 33 of the Daimlers at the end of the unwanted MET order to run a service in London in association with the LGOC; 27 of these buses were commandeered by the War Office, 23 of them were converted to lorries. They were replaced during 1915 and 1916 by Daimler chassis transferred from other subsidiaries of the parent company, British Electric Traction (BET). Some of these buses came from the Northern General Transport Company and the Potteries Motor Traction Company.[10] By these and other expedients, 272 additional buses had been added to the bus fleet of the capital. There was a shortage of bus crews as more and more men volunteered for military service.

Women were taken on as 'substitute' mechanics, conductors and cleaners. They were later to be dismissed as men returned from the war. Petrol shortages then began to reduce the number of buses that could be run. The older types of bus were taken out of service again An experiment was made to fuel a double-decker bus with coal gas contained in a 'balloon' gas bag carried on the upper deck. It was quite successful while the reservoir was full but as the gas was used up the empty bag caught the wind and blew about like a loose sail. In August 1918 twenty B-type buses were fitted with coal gas cylinders fitted on each side of the lower deck below the longitudinal benches and the unsuspecting passengers. A small petrol tank was kept for starting.

A group of 436 members of the LGOC were sworn in as special constables and one third of these were on call at any given time. At short notice a fleet of 100 omnibuses could be made available to transport special constables to deal with air raid damage. The special constables in London during the war acted not only policemen but as many as ten per cent of them were trained in first aid and many more in salvage and rescue work, the sort of duties called Air Raid Precautions (ARP) in the Second World War.

On Saturday 7 July 1917, 30 German heavy Gotha bombers attacked London in a daylight raid. Hundreds of special constables were collected from the police stations across London by bus and despatched to the East End where the damage was at its worst. Although the streets were blocked by traffic and sightseers the buses got through very quickly.

On 11 November 1918 the Armistice was announced. People crowded onto the streets of London to celebrate. Soldiers and sailors in uniform were feted and hauled on to the tops of cars, taxis and buses to celebrate the end of the war. A medical student who was at King's College in the Strand described seeing elderly City gents in black coats and pin-striped trousers beating on the direction boards of the buses like drums. One such drummer was the American poet Ezra Pound, who was seen beating on the side of a bus with his stick; happier at the end of this war than the next (he was accused of treason in 1945 for his support of the Fascists).

Australian and Canadian soldiers started a fire at the foot of Nelson's Column in Trafalgar Square, using the billboards around its foot bearing the slogan 'Buy War Bonds', and when this supply of fuel ran low they supplemented it with the destination boards from buses brought to a standstill by the crowds. The heat damage to the granite base of the Column can still be seen as a reminder of the first Armistice Day celebrations.

1   *Commercial Motor* 17 September 1914, p50.

2   H. E. Boisseau *The Prudential Staff and the Great War*. London: Prudential Assurance Co., 1938.

3   Guides at the Pavilion still tell the story of an unconscious Indian soldier who woke in one of the fabulous rooms of the Pavilion, convinced he had reached paradise.

4   D. H. Lawrence, in a letter to Lady Ottoline Morrell, dated 9 September 1915. Quoted in: Samuel Hynes. *A War Imagined: The First World War and English Culture*. London: The Bodley Head, 1990.

5   Wilbur Cross. *Zeppelins of World War 1*. London: I B Tauris, 1991.

6   Nigel Steel and Peter Hart. *Tumult in the clouds: the British experience of war in the air, 1914-1918*. London: Hodder & Stoughton, 1997.

7   *London Evening News*. 26 February 1925.

8   Chris and Ken Adam [military editor Ian Hook]. *1914-1918: a village remembers: military and social history: letters, diaries, photographs from Faulkbourne in Essex*. Witham: Faulkbourne, 1999.

9   Michael MacDonagh, the Younger. *In London during the Great War*. The diary of a journalist. London: Eyre & Spottiswoode, 1935.

10   G Robbins. *London Historical Research Group Bulletin No. 109*. Omnibus Society, 1992.

Aprés la guerre fini,
Tous les soldats parti,
Mademoiselle avec petit bébé,
Aprés la guerre fini.

Soldier's-French song of the First
World War sung to the tune of *Under
the Bridges of Paris*.

APRÉS LA GUERRE FINI: WAR BUSES IN PEACETIME

'Aprés la guerre fini' was a phrase used during the war to mean any time impossibly far in the future. The fighting came to an end rather unexpectedly on 11 November 1918, although top level Allied planning was preparing for the war to continue into 1919. The plan was to launch a massive assault on the German lines with hundreds of new tanks and the big new American army, which was fast approaching its peak of fitness and training. The attack at the Battle of Amiens in October 1918, spearheaded by the Canadians carried to Villers-Bretonneux by the Auxiliary (Omnibus) Park, had exposed the underlying weakness of the German army and demonstrated its declining morale. The German army began a hurried retreat to the Rhine. The buses helped the Allied armies to follow. On 10 November 1918, the 2nd Middlesex, a battalion of the First Army, travelled by bus for seven hours and then marched twenty-seven miles to enable them to reach Mons, the place where they had begun their war in 1914.

After the Armistice the buses began to carry the men home for demobilisation. On 31 December 1918, Dr. Dunn and the 2nd Royal Welch Fusiliers were taken back by bus across the devastated areas of the old Somme battlefields to Villers-Bretonneux. By December 1918 the bus services in London were suffering from the accumulated shortages of vehicles, staff and petrol. Public complaints about the service were becoming increasingly frequent.[1] The LGOC issued a statement in December 1918 saying that it had 200 spare buses that it could put on the road if petrol was released by the Petrol Control Department of the British Government, and the company was applying for release of its old staff from the armed services as a matter of priority. On 6 January 1919 a group of 150 Army Service Corps drivers, mostly former London bus men (and therefore strongly unionized before the war) left their camp at Osterley Park, without permission, and drove in three lorries to call on the Prime

Minister, Lloyd George. They were met by an officer of the Demobilisation Department who assured them of their rapid release, after 8 January.[2]

The first year of peace still meant shortages and problems. On Monday 3 February 1919, a strike on the London Underground took place in a dispute about working hours. Traffic jammed up throughout London as the travelling public rushed for alternative transport. On Wednesday 5 February, two motor buses, which had just returned from France, were used to bring War Office staff into work. The buses were painted black and the crews were still in khaki. These buses were further supplemented by a large number of army lorries, which offered a free service to the public. Although no fares were charged many crew members were noticed to have bulging pockets as they were given the fares by passengers who insisted on paying.

The Traffic Emergency buses

By 24 February 1919, another 100 buses were transferred from the Government War Department to the LGOC for passenger use. This was still not enough to cope with the demand. The Metropolitan Police Licensing Authority was persuaded to relax, temporarily, its stringent conditions for licensing of public stage carriage vehicles, provided they were labelled as 'Traffic Emergency Vehicles'. These buses, still in khaki-green paint were quickly put into service.

On Saturday 31 May 1919, *The Times* had a headline 'Lorry-Omnibuses On Monday' and the first, still in service khaki-green with the W↑D signs on its sides, went into service on route 33 between Barnes and Charing Cross. Altogether 180 lorries, all AEC Y-types, were taken from the Surplus Government Property Disposal Board in June 1919. They had quickly been adapted for their civilian role by fitting plain wooden benched cross-wise

Opposite
Chassis returned from the Front, 1919.
1998/36594

and a stair was built at the rear using the tailboard in its construction. Slatted life-guards were fitted between the front and rear wheels and a safety board was fitted to each side of the lorry to keep passenger's arms safely inside the vehicle.

Paper route notices were pasted on each side together with the GENERAL fleetname of the LGOC and the words 'Traffic Emergency Bus' on the near side only. The vehicles were licensed to carry 27 passengers with no standing allowed. They had started work in the summer but were not popular and often travelled only partly full. The only time they were really appreciated was during the national railway strike, from 26 September to 5 October 1919. Lorry-buses ran at a financial loss as the 45hp Tylor engine of a Y-type used petrol at 4½ mpg and the vehicle could only carry 27 passengers whilst a B-type bus could do 7 mpg and carry 34 passengers. Finally the Board of Trade paid the LGOC £9,000 to compensate them for the extra costs of operating them.[3]

A large number of ex-army vehicles were brought back from France and stored in very muddy conditions on Kempton Park racecourse, Middlesex, to be made available for sale.[4] The LGOC was managing to increase its supply of buses. A final batch of 250 B-types was built between December 1918 and April 1919. Some of these buses used the American components and this required further negotiation with the Metropolitan Police to license the heavier vehicles. As B-type vehicles were released by the War Department they were put into service. A group of 165 vehicles that had served only at home was felt to be in sufficiently good condition to be fitted with bodies from store and put back into use as normal vehicles. After the agreement to allow temporary sub-standard vehicles to be licensed, another 250 buses were bought back from the War Department as they returned from overseas. From May 1919 these were introduced as khaki Traffic Emergency buses.[5] Most had had only a limited overhaul to replace the missing windows and damaged seats.

Another 100 red Traffic Emergency buses, including B43 'Ole Bill', were also introduced, with passenger bodies from storage fitted to substandard chassis. Some of these bodies were from old Straker-Squires and MET Daimlers. Four ex-army B-type lorries, B2850, B2852, B2855 and B2857, were fitted with single-deck bodies to work the Blackwall Tunnel route. When the National bus company sold off its steam buses the LGOC bought 78 of the bodies, which were painted khaki and mounted on B-type chassis. In total, 210 khaki emergency buses were eventually licensed, together with 94 red emergency buses.

By June 1920 most of the Traffic Emergency buses were being upgraded as their turn came for overhaul. The new 46-seat K-type bus was being introduced into service and as the bus supply situation eased the emergency buses were withdrawn, the last one serving into the summer of 1921.[6] By the beginning of 1926 only 214 B-type buses were still licensed in London.

They were scattered between 25 garages where they served as spare vehicles in case of breakdowns. These buses were to provide one last public service. The Trades Union Congress called a General Strike of all its members on 3 May 1926 in support of the coal miners. The railways and most tram and bus services stopped at once. The LGOC concentrated all its remaining B-types at the Chiswick Garage in west London under military guard. Volunteers came from all walks of life and offered to drive the buses. To protect them from militant strikers the bonnets were draped in barbed wire and a policeman sat on the front seat next to the driver. Improvised bus depots were set up in the Royal Parks, which were guarded by soldiers. Four circular bus routes were organized. The buses were by now of negligible book value and the LGOC no doubt felt that any damage done to them, either by the strikers or by the amateur drivers, could be borne with equanimity. One Tilling-Stevens petro-electric bus was attacked and overturned by strikers. The B-types seem to have escaped major harm. The last B-types in service were used by the LGOC for staff transport until March 1929.

Many B-types were sold by the LGOC to other operators in Britain and, by 1922, one could be bought in running order for £100. Several ex-army drivers set up their own bus services with their army gratuities. The LGOC insisted, as a condition of the sale, that they could not be operated within thirty miles of London. At least thirty-four were sold to Australia and, almost unbelievably, one of these was driven from an outback farm to Melbourne in 1972 to take advantage of a part-exchange offer.[7] The narrative of the B-type did not end after it ceased operation as a motor vehicle. Bodies were separated from chassis and sold off as cheap summer houses, to be deposited on small plots of land by impoverished holidaymakers around the Sussex, Kent and Essex coasts.

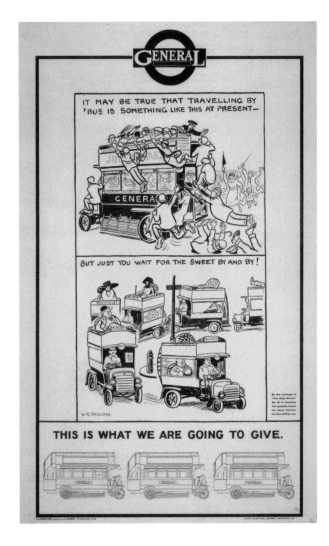

Top Left
One of a series of posters acknowledging post-war problems and promising a brighter future, published early in 1920.
1983/4/888

Top right
Pre-war Y-type bus, relicensed and pressed into service as a Traffic Emergency Bus, 1919.
1998/71508

Left
B-type in Athens, still in LGOC livery, c1918.
1998/36571

1   G J Robbins & J B Atkinson. *The London B-type motor omnibus*. Twickenham: DPR Marketing and Sales The World of Transport, 1991, p 1.

2   Ian F W Beckett and Keith Simpson [eds.]. *A Nation in arms: a social history of the British Army in the First World War*. Manchester: Manchester University Press, c1985.

3   J D P House & G Robbins. *Traffic Emergency 1919: a study in improvisation*. Streatham: The Omnibus Society, c1970s, p9.

4   The vehicles were later moved to Slough, Berkshire, so that the racecourse could be reopened.

5   J D P House & G Robbins. *Traffic Emergency 1919: a study in improvisation*. Streatham: The Omnibus Society, c1970s, p9.

6   Records suggest that the lorry-buses were returned to the Government by the LGOC from late 1919, and that from March 1920 many of them were repurchased by the stand-alone vehicle manufacturing business AEC, which had been created by the LGOC to build its buses.

7   G J Robbins & J B Atkinson. *The London B-type motor omnibus*. Twickenham: DPR Marketing and Sales The World of Transport, 1991, p106.

1st

2nd

15th

ONE PENNY
1914
PENNY ALL THE WAY

16th

18th

50th

There are very real problems about determining the colour schemes and markings of First World War vehicles. No one dreamt that anyone in the future might be interested in such a subject as what colour a bus was painted. Records are very fragmentary. Human beings do not have a very good colour memory; nor do we have a very good vocabulary to describe it. Much of the available information comes from black and white photographs, and it can be difficult to interpret shades of grey in monochrome images. Typically, black and white film at that time tended to make blue appear too light whilst red appeared almost black. The official censor did not help when markings were blotted out that might give information to the enemy. Photographers were accustomed to retouch their pictures heavily to make them suitable for newspaper reproduction and they often added inscriptions to the negative. Photographic captions are sometimes wrong, even at some important sources such as the Imperial War Museum. In summary then, any description given here is inevitably incomplete and is also very subjective. Any opinions are my own and I am ready to stand corrected if other evidence should be offered.

The single-deck B-type bus-ambulances seem only to have served in Britain and they all appear to be in the original LGOC bright red colour. The General signs on each side of the bus were in gold and were applied in the form of a transfer. The only military changes visible were the white painted windows and the Red Cross signs on the windows.

The Daimler buses that went to Belgium and France in 1914 were at first in the royal blue livery common to both the MET and Gearless companies, with white painted window frames. The MET Insignia on the sides was in light blue, edged with gold. The Gearless fleet name appears to be very similar. The only military additions

were large chalked numbers on the front such as 17 and 19, 19th Batt. and one example, on D185, of a chalked name 'HOWE' - the name of one of the naval battalions of the Royal Naval Division. Once the buses had returned from Antwerp they were painted, on 4 November 1914, a colour which from photographs appears to be a darker shade than the khaki later used by the Army. It has been described as dark-green in various accounts: 'At last the old dark-green buses rolled up...our driver had been at Antwerp'[1], and 'for the buses are painted a neutral green all over: but the conductor is always ready and willing to tell you what his previous route was...That Daimler behind you is one of the Number Nineteens'[2].

The Royal Marine Anti-Aircraft Brigade's Pierce Arrow 2-pounder Pom-Pom armoured cars were painted a colour described as Daimler Khaki-green.[3] This may describe the colour used on the buses. To this were added the white stencilled letters RND on the front, back and sides. On some examples the civilian number plate was also stencilled RND. Individual numbers for each bus were added from 1 to 40 on the front and back. By August 1915 the buses had been taken over by the Army as 16th Auxiliary Omnibus Coy, and seem to have been painted the same colour as other military buses - probably khaki - together with the W↑D number in white on each side of the bonnet and on the rear of the vehicle. This number (for example ↑2224 for a bus of the 1st Auxiliary Omnibus Coy) was painted in white numbers, 6 inches high and ½ inch wide; a broad arrow was placed either above or in front of the number and it was applied to three places, one on each bonnet cover and one at the back of the vehicle. In addition each vehicle usually carried high on the front and back, the number of the individual bus in the column

Each B-type bus still displayed the old LGOC B-type number on the bonnet, which as it was made up of riveted numbers on a plate, shows easily on some old photos even though it was painted over. Riveted letters were also used to mark the chassis on each side just below the driver. Daimlers had their number painted on the bonnet, so these figures did not show after the transfer into grey or khaki.

The B-types of the 1st Auxiliary Omnibus Coy went to France in unchanged LGOC red. After a few weeks they were painted a less easily discernible colour by their own crews: this was probably a khaki-green. Eye witnesses give a fairly wide variety of colours in their descriptions:

May 1915: 'green painted London buses took the 11th Batt. towards Ypres'. Private. W Jaeger, King's.
Jan 1916: 'LGO Coys buses painted service green'. Lieutenant P D Ravenscroft, KRRC.
July 1916: 'old London buses disguised with drab paint'. Lieutenant. E Blunden, 11th Royal Sussex Regiment
July 1916: 'three and a half hours ride (in a green London bus)'. The Reverend Julian Bickersteth.
July 1916: 'London General Omnibus Company's double-deckers, their once gay vermilion saddened to a mud-colour'. Captain Henry Ogle MC, 7th Royal Warwicks.
Jan 1917: 'LGOC's buses, their red painted khaki of sorts'. Captain J C Dunn, RAMC.

A lot of observers comment on the fact that the khaki paint was often chipped and the old red colour would show through: 'here and there, where the drab khaki of their wartime paint was chipped, a glint of red still hinted of the days when they had plied along Oxford Street, travelling north to Kilburn, or honked through Piccadilly and south to Kensington. The official formula for 'service green' paint used yellow ochre and lamp black.[4] This mixture gives a brownish colour. The pigments were stirred into linseed oil to make the paint, and the oil added a greenish tinge, which varied considerably with

the age of the linseed oil and whether it had been stored in the dark or in sunlight. This may explain the shade variations noted above.

There is also some evidence that certain vehicles may have been painted grey. Private Darby of 46 Coy MT describes when he left Grove Park in his bus, 'and took on board some large drums of grey paint'.[5] Other recollections add to the evidence of grey painted buses: 'We all went in London omnibuses. They are painted grey'.[6] In *Cambrai*, A J Smithers remembered 'the buses, genuine solid tyred London General Omnibus Company, painted grey'.[7] H Williamson noted 'the grey - once London red – motor-buses, their windows boarded up' in *The Patriot's Progress*.[8]

The Auxiliary Omnibus Company unit signs

In order to organize and account for each of the large number of buses, lorries and other vehicles operated by the Army Service Corps, and the army generally, numbers and other identifying marks were added to the basic colour schemes of khaki or grey. At first these were just simple text panels such as '91 Coy MT ASC', painted on the side of the vehicles together with the W↑D sign of the War Department. It was subsequently realised that this explicit labelling made it too easy for enemy spies to identify units: special pictorial signs were substituted from mid-1916. These are described below.

1st Auxiliary Omnibus Company

This Coy used a flying wheel emblem in black on a white square, presumably derived directly from the original London General Omnibus Company symbol used for staff cap badges. D V Lewis drew the badge of his company in his record. He states that it was stencilled on the front and the back of the buses and on the front of the lorries. It appears in the drawing *"Penny all the Way"* by Adrian Hill, and, slightly obscured, in the photograph from the

Imperial War Museum, painted on the back of the bus beside the destination board space.[9]

2nd Auxiliary Omnibus Company

The sign for this Coy was a black arrow on a white rectangle. Each bus had four such signs: one on the front with the arrow facing to the left hand side of the bus, one on each lower side with the arrow facing forward and one at the back on the stair panel facing upwards at 45 degrees. It appeared on the tailboard and the front of the dashboard of the Coy's lorries. I have been unable to find any reason for the choice of this emblem but it does occur as a common theme in motorized units. It may have some reference to the old Arrow London bus company as the design of the arrow is exactly that used by that company before it was taken over by Vanguard. For examples see IWM photos E (Aus)1105, E(Aus)1106, E(Aus)8012 and E(Aus)1829. It is also seen on Tank Museum photos including 2304/A5.[10]

15th Auxiliary Omnibus Company

This company chose as their emblem a small sitting black dog in a white circle. A photograph of this company's Locomobile buses shows a small white dog sitting on the bonnet of one vehicle. It looks like a bull terrier and may be the unit's mascot and the inspiration for their sign.

16th Auxiliary Omnibus Company

This unit's sign was, aptly for a former naval unit, the Britannia one penny coin, accompanied by the motto 'All the Way'. The advertising slogan 'Penny All The Way' was one used back in horse-bus days which somehow had caught the public imagination, and was remembered long after prices had risen. It appears on the Imperial War Museum photographs Q3022 and CO965. The sign was described by Lance Corporal Gower, a driver of the 16th Auxiliary Omnibus Coy, in a letter archived at the Imperial

War Museum, and he confirms that it was painted on the sides of the buses.[11] Captain J C Dunn also mentions it in his book: 'The Transport Company's sign is the reverse of a penny and the motto 'All the Way.' It would have first prize from me among the many signs I've seen'.[12]

18th Auxiliary Omnibus Company

This sign had an unusual origin. The unit was originally equipped with American Locomobile lorries converted into troop carriers. Some of these vehicles had been bought in the United States - before it entered the war - by the German government, but the neutral ship carrying them had been intercepted by the British naval blockade and the vehicles confiscated. When unit signs were being adopted it was suggested that as these lorries intended for Germany had all been performing such sterling war service, the Kaiser might like to recognize it by awarding them all the Iron Cross (a German military award). The unit sign was therefore a white German cross. No pictures seem to exist to show where this was applied to the vehicles.

50th Auxiliary Omnibus Company

This was the headquarters company, and had as its sign a black elephant on a red circle. There is a photograph I have seen of its use on a poster advertising the unit's cinema, which was powered by the generator on their workshop lorry. The elephant was probably chosen to symbolise their transport of heavy loads in their Ammunition Column days. One photograph shows the red disc with a black elephant with a white tusk and a white II beneath it. Alongside to the right seems to be the rectangular badge of the Third Army, three stripes horizontally of red, black and red with a white circle on it. These signs were painted on the side of the bus below the windows.

51st Auxiliary Omnibus Company

This unit's sign was a ring of two intertwined red and

white bands resembling a rope, on a black ground. I have only seen this emblem on the Company Christmas card for 1918, sent by Driver J A Stuart, so I am unable to describe its use on vehicles.

On top of all the official signs the troops being carried would add comments of their own. There was a lot of chalk in the Somme countryside and they sometimes could not resist adding graffitti on the tempting blank sides of the boards which replaced the lower windows. Tom Green recorded one in his diary which made him laugh: 'the bus, not a bit of glass but a long board with the words written in bold letters, "I have no pane, dear mother now"'.[13]

The Auxiliary Omnibus Companies Association

One final piece of insignia carried on B43 Ole Bill, although not a wartime one, is the motif still displayed on the bus upper deck sides and rear. It is a circular shape bearing a representation of the Ole Bill bus, with the letters AOCA and 1914 on pentagons around it, and the names of notable 'battle honours' Antwerp, Ypres, Loos, Somme and Amiens. This design represents the veterans' association of men who had served with the Army Service Corps Omnibus Coys in France and Belgium. With this motif we end our journey as we began, because for many years the AOCA men paraded with AEC B-Type motor bus Ole Bill to the Cenotaph, for each Armistice Day commemoration.

1   W H L Watson. *Adventures of a Despatch Rider*. Edinburgh; London: W Blackwood & Sons, 1915, p222.

2   Ian Hay [John Hay Beith]. *Carrying On: After The First Hundred Thousand*. Edinburgh: William Blackwood and Sons, 1917, p 19.

3   B T White. *British Tank Markings and Names: The Unit Markings, Individual Names and Paint Colours of British Armoured Fighting Vehicles, 1914-1945*. London: Arms & Armour Press.

4   Lyn MacDonald. *Somme*. London: Penguin Books, 1993, p. 90.

5   Private Edward James Darby M1/6948, 46 Coy ASC-MT, 2nd Cavalry Division, BEF. '*How to become a Soldier*' in one month. [Manuscript.] London Transport Museum Library reference B061, Box 1.

6   The Rev David Railton, attached 18th Northumberland Fusiliers, quoted in: Michael Moynihan [ed.]. *God On Our Side: The British Padre in World War I*. London: Leo Cooper / Secker & Warburg, 1983.

7   A J Smithers. *Cambrai: The First Great Tank Battle 1917*. London: Leo Cooper, 1992, p 135.

8   Henry Williamson. *The Patriot's Progress*. London: Sphere, 1978.

9   'London motor omnibuses drawn up on the Cassel-Dunkerque road, 8th August 1917'. Photograph by Lieutenant Ernest Brooks. Imperial War Museum reference Q2690.

10 For examples see IWM photos E (Aus)1105, E(Aus)1106, E(Aus)8012 and E(Aus)1829. It is also seen on The Tank Museum (Bovington) photographs including reference 2304-A5.

11 Lance Corporal F Gower M2/082418, 16th Auxiliary Bus Company ASC, in a letter of 2 June 1965. Manuscript in collection of Imperial War Museum reference Documents.867. See: http://www.iwm.org.uk/collections/item/object/1030001338 [accessed 18 June 2014].

12 Captain J C Dunn. *The War the Infantry Knew 1914-1919. A Chronicle of Service in France and Belgium with The Second Battalion His Majesty's Twenty-Third Foot, The Royal Welch Fusiliers: founded on personal records, recollections and reflections, assembled, edited and partly written by One of their Medical Officers*. London: P S King & Son, 1938, p 380.

13 Extract from 'Tom Green's Journal' quoted in: Colin Walsh. *Mud, Songs and Blighty: A Scrapbook of the First World War*. London: Hutchinson, 1975.

Three B-type buses are preserved in museums. Each of these has been heavily restored and it is very difficult to know how much of each bus is original. After the First World War the system of overhauls at each individual garage, a process taking sixteen days, was changed to a production line process at the Chiswick works, which only took four days.[1] When each bus came into Chiswick for a major overhaul it was stripped to the bare chassis. The body, engine and transmission were taken off to their own overhaul department. After inspection and repair, the chassis were put back into line and any part that was ready was put onto the chassis so that a bus, in its career, might have several different bodies, engines, wheels, and radiators.

B43 (LN4743) bore its first body to France in October 1914. In 1919 it was fitted with a body which had been placed in storage during the conflict, and served as a red 'Traffic Emergency Bus.' It then had a further replacement body fitted and was given to the Auxiliary Omnibus Association.

B214 (LA9802) also served in France, but as a lorry. When it returned to England in 1919 the LGOC thought it was not worth their while to buy it back. A man called Hinton bought B214 and drove it to Chelmsford where the old National steam buses were being broken up. He fitted it with one of their old steam bus bodies. With this vehicle and another complete B-type that he subsequently bought from the LGOC, he started the Laindon and District Motor Service. After Hinton died the chassis and body were used for many years as a tool shed; when it was discovered parts from several B-types were used to repair the chassis, but the body was beyond repair. Initially a single-deck body, built in 1921 and used on B5103, was used to rebuild it. When another complete B-type body was found, being used as a garden shed, this was refurbished and the vehicle was rebuilt as new. It is now in a Dutch motor museum.

Above
Restored B-type B2737 at Finsbury Park, 2014.
Martin Tulloch

B340 (LA9928) was one of the buses that was only used on the home front and was repurchased by the LGOC in 1916. It was then fitted with one of the three panelled bodies that had first been introduced in 1914 but, being new, were all taken off and put in store. When B340 was taken out of service in December 1924, it was chosen as the B-type bus for preservation by the Company and used occasionally on private charters. It was exhibited in the Museum of British Transport at Clapham from 1963, at Syon Park from 1972 and is now in the collection of the London Transport Museum.

London Transport Museum in Covent Garden has been able to mark the centenary of the first use of military buses in 1914 by restoring parts from several chassis to make up B2737 in its LGOC livery. In autumn 2014 it will be transformed into wartime appearance, with military colours and markings and make a commemorative return to its former haunts in northern France and Belgium.

There are some other B-type bus chassis awaiting restoration. One was in a container in the West Country. The owner also had a Daimler chassis. B237 (LA9825) has been recovered from New Zealand and is in a Yorkshire museum awaiting full restoration. There is a Tilling-Stevens petro-electric chassis in Colchester, fitted with an incomplete 'British' Daimler body, but this was recently sold on.

Surprisingly, there is still a 1907 Milnes-Daimler bus, LN314, preserved at the Mercedes-Benz Museum in Stuttgart. This bus was built on a Daimler Motoren Gesellschaft chassis from Canstatt, in Württemburg in Germany. The body was built by UEC of Preston, now part of GEC. This bus served with the London Motor Omnibus Company's Vanguard fleet. It was restored by Richard Peskett, who has now restored the Battlebus (B2737) for the London Transport Museum. Eight buses just like this took part in the Shoeburyness run in 1909. Although the history of this bus is not known with certainty, it is possible that it may have taken part in the historic trials as one of the eight vehicles.

There are a number of models of B-types in museums. A beautiful study of B2029 is in the Science Museum in South Kensington, but this is a model of a special experimental body with opening windows, and another in the Imperial War Museum collection'.[2] The model was a gift from London Transport and made by apprentices at Chiswick Works.

1   The LGOC had moved the works to Chiswick from Walthamstow. It had to provide a free bus service for its workers living in east London to get to work – a journey a friend of my father's, who worked for London Transport, was still making in the 1960's.
2   Incorrectly wearing the Britannia Penny badge of the 16th Auxiliary Omnibus Company who only used Daimlers.

GLOSSARY OF SPECIALIST TERMS

AEC	Associated Equipment Company
ASC	Army Service Corps
Billet	a place to sleep
Column	a line of vehicles
Coy	British Army abbreviation of Company
'Diff'	differential - the mechanism forming part of the rear axle of a B-Type bus, transferring power from the engine and gearbox to the rear wheels
Ditched	a vehicle which has veered off the roadway
Debuss	unload troops from a bus or buses
DSM	Distinguished Service Medal
Embuss	load troops onto a bus or buses
Enfilade	A volley of gunfire directed along a line from end to end
hp	horse power
Impressment	a term historically applied to the forcible taking of men into the armed services, particularly the Navy
KRRC	King's Royal Rifle Corps
NCO	Non-commissioned officer

FURTHER READING

Beckett, Ian F W, and Keith Simpson [eds.].
A Nation in arms: a social history of the British Army in the First World War. Manchester: Manchester University Press, c1985.

Blacker, K C, R S Lunn and R G Westgate. *London's Buses: Volume One: The Independent Era 1922-1934*. St Albans: H J Publications, 1977.

Coppard, George. With a machine gun to Cambrai: the tale of a young Tommy in Kitchener's army 1914-1918. London: H M S O, 1969.

Crosland, T W H. *The Collected Poems of T W H Crosland*. London: Martin Secker, 1917.
Cross, Wilbur. Zeppelins of World War 1. London: I B Tauris, 1991.

Crawley, R J, D R MacGregor and F D Simpson. *The years between 1909-1969: Vol. 1: The National Story to 1929*. Hedingham: D R MacGregor, 1979.

Dunn, Captain J C. *The War the Infantry Knew 1914-1919. A Chronicle of Service in France and Belgium with The Second Battalion His Majesty's Twenty-Third Foot, The Royal Welch Fusiliers: founded on personal records, recollections and reflections, assembled, edited and partly written by One of their Medical Officers*. London: P S King & Son, 1938.

Glazier, Ken. *The Battles of the General: London Buses 1918-1929*. Harrow Weald: Capital Transport Publishing, 2003.

Hay, Ian [John Hay Beith]. *Carrying On: After The First Hundred Thousand*. Edinburgh: William Blackwood and Sons, 1917.

Hibbs, John. *The History of British Bus Services*. Newton Abbot: David and Charles, 1968.

House, J D P, & G Robbins. *Traffic Emergency 1919: a study in improvisation*. Streatham: The Omnibus Society, c1970s.

Jones, Daphne. *Bullets and bandsmen: the story of a bandsman on the Western Front / written by his daughter*. Downton: Owl Press, 1992.

Lee, Charles E. *The Early Motor Bus*, London: British Railways Board, 1964.

MacDonald, Lyn. *Somme*. London: Penguin Books, 1993.

Moynihan, Michael [ed.]. *God On Our Side: The British Padre in World War I*. London: Leo Cooper / Secker & Warburg, 1983.

Nalder, Major General R F H. *The Royal Corps of Signals: A history of its antecedents and development, circa 1800-1955*. London: Royal Signals Institution, 1958.

Osman, A H. Pigeons in the Great War. *A complete history of the Carrier Pigeon Service, 1914 to 1918*. London : "Racing Pigeon" Publishing Co., 1929.

Popham, Hugh. *The F.A.N.Y. in peace and war: the story of the First Aid Nursing Yeomanry 1907-2003*. Barnsley: Leo Cooper, 2003.

Robbins, G J, & J B Atkinson. *The London B-type motor omnibus*. Twickenham: DPR Marketing and Sales The World of Transport, 1991.

St Clair Stobart, Mabel Annie. *Miracles and Adventures: an autobiography*. n p: Rider, 1935.

Samson, Air-Commodore Charles Rumney. *Fights and flights*. London: Benn, 1930.

Sassoon, Siegfried. Memoirs of an Infantry Officer. By the author of Memoirs of a Fox-Hunting Man. London: Faber & Faber, 1930.

Shephard. Ernest [eds. *Bruce Rossor with Richard Holmes]. A Sergeant-Major's War: from Hill 60 to the Somme*. Marlborough: The Crowood Press in association with Anthony Bird, 1987.

Smithers, A J. *Cambrai: The First Great Tank Battle 1917*. London: Leo Cooper, 1992.

Steel, Nigel, and Peter Hart. *Tumult in the clouds: the British experience of war in the air, 1914-1918*. London: Hodder & Stoughton, 1997.

Thackray, Brian. *The AEC Story: Part One*. Glossop: Venture Publications, 2001.

Thackray, Brian. *A.E.C. Vehicles: Origins to 1929*. Glossop: Venture Publications, 2004.

Tomlinson, H M. *Waiting for Daylight*. London: Cassell & Co., 1922.

Vaughan, E C [with a foreword by John Terraine]. *Some desperate glory: the diary of a young officer, 1917*. London: Frederick Warne, 1982.

Walsh, Colin. *Mud, Songs and Blighty: A Scrapbook of the First World War*. London: Hutchinson, 1975.

Ward, Irene. *F.A.N.Y. Invicta*. London: Hutchinson, 1955.

Watson, W H L. *Adventures of a Despatch Rider*. Edinburgh; London: W Blackwood & Sons, 1915.

White, B T. *British Tank Markings and Names: The Unit Markings, Individual Names and Paint Colours of British Armoured Fighting Vehicles, 1914-1945*. London: Arms & Armour Press.

Williamson, Henry. *The Patriot's Progress*. London: Sphere, 1978.

Young, Michael. *Army Service Corps, 1902-1918*. London: Leo Cooper, 2000.

INDEX

1st GHQ Ammunition Park	42, 47, 49, 58, 59	B2737 B-type bus	106, 107
4 GHQ Ammunition Park	42, 50, 76 n2	Bailleul, France	39, 49, 59
7 GHQ Ammunition Park	50, 51, 58, 59, 74	Bairnsfather, Bruce	4, 16 n2
46 Company MT (Army Service Corps)	50, 51, 58, 59	Beattie, Captain M (Army Service Corps)	50
588 Company MT Army Service Corps	51	Belgian Army	30, 36
Admiralty	19	Belgian Field hospital, Antwerp	32
Advertising on buses	92	Benham, Dr Alice	36
Allott, Captain E H (Army Service Corps)	102	Benn, Captain (Army Service Corps)	50
ambulances, B-type, colour schemes	88	Berna (vehicle manufacturer)	58, 67
ambulances, buses used as	85	Bignall-Wild, Captain R K	8
American YMCA	59, 63	Blackwall Tunnel, London	24, 98
Amiens, France, Auxiliary (Omnibus) Park	96	British Bus Company (bus fleet operator)	92
Amiens, France, Battle of	32	British Daimler Company (vehicle manufacturer)	14
Antwerp, British advance to, in bus convoy	32, 36	British Electric Traction (bus fleet operator)	92
Antwerp, British retreat from, in bus convoy	32, 33, 35, 36, 38	British Field Hospital, Antwerp	32
Armistice (11 November 1918)	92, 93, 96	Brooke, Rupert	35
Armistice Day parade	96	Brown-Hughes & Strachan (vehicle manufacturer)	72
Army Service Corps Auxiliary Omnibus Companies		B-type ambulance colour schemes	102
1st Auxiliary Omnibus Company	42, 43, 46, 47, 48, 54	B-type bus	
	n3, 56, 62, 63, 101, 102	body alterations	25, 26 n4
2nd Auxiliary Omnibus Company	42, 47, 49, 54 n12, 62,	body fitted to other chassis	52, 84, 98
	101, 104	construction	18
3rd Auxiliary Omnibus Company	42, 50, 58, 67	converted for use as lorry	20, 21, 22, 30, 42, 50,
4th Auxiliary Omnibus Company	42, 50, 76 n2		78, 85
15th Auxiliary Omnibus Company	50, 51, 54 n17, 62, 74,	end of use in London	98
	101, 104	interior	19
16th Auxiliary Omnibus Company	39, 47, 51, 54 n18, 58,	maintenance in wartime	3, 50
	59, 72, 74, 101, 102,	mechanical features	18
	104, 107 n2	painting of	19
18th Auxiliary Omnibus Company	51, 54 n19, 62, 101, 104	post-war disposal for other uses	25, 90, 99
50th Auxiliary Omnibus Company	50, 51, 58, 59, 62, 101, 104	post-war manufacture of	98
51st Auxiliary Omnibus Company	50, 54 n16, 58, 62, 63, 104	seating arrangements	19
93 Company Army Service Corps	76 n2	single deck version	24
339 Company Army Service Corps	50, 58	single deck version, as ambulance	23, 24, 25
Arrow (bus fleet operator)	11	standardization of	18, 22
Ashfield, Lord (Albert Stanley)	14, 91	service in other cities	46
Associated Equipment Company (AEC)	13, 18, 43, 84, 85	B-type chassis 'American'	85
Association of Registered Medical Women	36	B-type chassis converted for other war uses	
Automobile Association	11	3-pounder gun lorries	80, 81
Auxiliary Company (MT), Army of the Rhine	63	13 pounder anti-aircraft gun lorries	81, 82, 84
Auxiliary Omnibus Companies Association	4, 105	water tankers	72
Auxiliary (Omnibus) Park MT	47, 50, 51, 56, 59, 62, 63	'Russian'	85
B43 'Ole Bill' B-type bus	4, 98, 105, 106	B-type vehicle, armoured	78, 79, 80
B214 B-type bus	106, 107	B-type lorry, armoured (War Office pattern)	78
B340 B-type bus	92, 107	B-type lorry, pre-war production	84

Buckingham Palace   4

Bulford Camp   50

bus body and chassis interchangeability   84

bus conductress   91

bus design, standardization   12

bus destination boards, London   19, 24

bus drivers, training for war service   45

Bus House Military Cemetery, St. Eloi, Belgium   47

bus passengers, queuing arrangements   19

bus service in wartime, organisation of troop movements   59, 61, 62

bus workers, London, recruitment for war service   30

bus, Clarkson steam   8, 10, 11

bus, De Dion   8

bus, K-type   98

bus, Milnes-Daimler   8

bus, Straker-Squire   8

buses converted for other war uses

        ambulances   74, 75, 88

        cavalry wireless units   66

        charabancs   58, 67

        mobile pigeon lofts   67, 70, 71, 72, 73

        mobile workshops   66, 67, 85

        searchlight lorries   67

        single-deck vehicles   75

        store lorries   67

buses for war service

        colour schemes   47, 102, 103, 107

        graffiti marking by troops   105

        requisitioning   11

        salvage of parts   85, 95

buses, home front service in wartime   87, 88

buses, post-war return to work in London   96, 97

buses, preserved vehicles   106

buses, service outside London   107

buses, to transport military bands   72, 74

buses, transferred for service in London   92

buses, use during London Underground workers' strike   96

buses, use for troop demobilisation   96

buses, use of for military troop transport ,trials   8, 9, 10, 11

Büssing (vehicle manufacturer)   22

Cameronian Regiment   37, 38

CC type bus (Daimler)   14

Cenotaph, London   4

Chiswick Garage, London   98

Chouffot, Sergeant Major Alfred   39, 47, 48

Churchill, Winston   28, 33, 38

Clarkson, Thomas   8, 9, 10, 11, 72

Clay Hall (bus garage)   16 n1

Daimler bus   13, 27, 29, 30, 31,
                                                             37, 38, 39, 42, 47,
                                                             65, 67, 78, 88, 92

        bus body fitted to B-type chassis   84

        captured by German army   34

        colour schemes   102

        converted for other war uses: anti-aircraft gun   83

        converted for other war uses: mobile bath unit   72

        converted to lorries   39, 83, 92

        sent for war service   88

        use in other cities and countries   39

Daimler lorry   28, 51, 68, 69, 84

'Daimler-Wolseley-Straker' type bus   12

Dalston (bus garage)   4

Darby, Private E J   50, 75

De Dion-Bouton (vehicle manufacturer)   12, 88, 90

demobilisation of troops   96

destination boards, London buses   19, 24, 46, 93

Douglas, Robert (London bus driver)   30, 43

Dumble, Captain Wilfred (Royal Engineers, Royal Marines)   30

Eastern National Bus company   11

female workers on transport system during wartime   91, 92

First Aid Nursing Yeomanry   72

First Essex (bus fleet operator)   11

Forest Gate (bus garage)   38

Forge et Chantiers de France   31, 78, 80

Fraser, Ivor   32

Gamwell, Hope   72

Gamwell, Marian   72

Garford (vehicle manufacturer)   72

Gearless (bus fleet operator)   14, 27, 40 n25, 84,
                                                             88, 102

Geddes, Sir Eric   56

General Strike (1926), emergency bus services   98

German Army, advance through Belgium   30, 35

Ghent, Belgium   31, 32, 35, 36, 38

Goodbye Piccadilly (exhibition)   4

Grove Park, London, Army Service Corps barracks   42, 44, 46, 47, 50,
                                                             85

Haig, General, later Field Marshal, Sir Douglas   56, 62

Hetherington, Flight Commander T G   78

Howell, Colonel G L H (Army Service Corps)   56, 59

Imperial War Museum — 4

Janson, Lieutenant S — 49

Kaiser Wilhelm II — 28

King George V — 4

Kitchener, Lord — 78

K-type bus — 98

Laindon and District Motor Service (bus fleet operator) — 107

Lewis, Driver D V (Army Service Corps) — 47, 56, 58

Leyland (vehicle manufacturer) — 90

Lloyd George, David — 96

Locomobile (vehicle manufacturer) — 50, 51, 52, 67

London Field Ambulance military band — 72, 74

London General Omnibus Company — 4, 8, 11, 12, 14, 15, 18, 20, 22, 24, 28, 39, 43, 47, 50, 88, 92, 96, 98, 107

    employees as special constables — 92

    Holloway vehicle body works — 18, 28, 83

    Private Hire department — 20

    vehicle livery — 24

London Road Car Company (bus fleet operator) — 8

London Transport Museum — 4, 92, 106, 107

London transport workers, recruitment for war service — 42

London, Zeppelin air raids on — 90, 92

L-type (chassis) — 90

Mahoney, Driver William (Army Service Corps) — 43, 56, 58

Maudslay (vehicle manufacturer) — 58, 67

Metropolitan Police Licensing Authority — 9, 12, 84, 96, 98

Milnes-Daimler (chassis) — 67, 80, 106

Montgomery, Lieutenant Bernard — 72

Mortlake (bus garage) — 11

Museum of British Transport, Clapham, London — 107

National (bus fleet operator) — 10, 11, 107

Northern General Transport Company (bus fleet operator) — 92

Old Ford (bus garage) — 4, 16 n1

Osterley Park, Middlesex (army service corps barracks and training ground) — 96

Peerless (vehicle manufacturer) — 50, 67

Peskett, Richard — 106

Pigeons, use of for communications in wartime — 67, 70, 71, 72

Potteries Motor Traction Company (bus fleet operator) — 92

Refugees, transported by bus in London — 89

Rouen, France — 46, 49, 75

Royal Air Force — 40 n1

Royal Army Medical Corps — 20, 46, 75

Royal Artillery — 58

Royal Automobile Club — 31

Royal British Legion Poppy Appeal — 4

Royal Flying Corps — 28, 38, 40 n1, 58

Royal Logistics Corps Museum, Surrey — 51, 80

Royal Naval Air Service — 28, 40 n1, 78, 80

Royal Naval Division — 29, 30, 32, 35, 37, 38, 39, 78, 102

Royal Naval Division, lorry livery — 83

Royal Naval Division, bus colour schemes — 102

Saint-Valery-sur-Somme, France — 47, 50, 51, 56, 58, 59

Salonika, Greece — 43, 45

Samson, Felix — 80

Samson, Lieutenant Commander Charles Rumney — 28, 31, 38, 78, 80, 81

Sauley, Captain A G (Army Service Corps) — 51, 62

Searle, Frank — 8, 9, 11, 12, 14, 18, 30, 84

Silent Knight sleeve valve engine — 14, 67

Society of Automobile Mechanics — 50

Southall and District Traction company (bus operator) — 25

St. Eloi, Belgium — 47, 48

St. Omer, France — 38, 39, 46, 51, 70

Straker-Squire (chassis) — 22, 67, 88, 98

Surplus Government Property Disposal Board — 96

Talbot armoured car — 78

Tank Corps — 62

Tilling-Stevens (vehicle manufacturer) — 67, 98

TOT (Underground group staff magazine) — 14, 30, 38, 43, 47

Traffic Emergency Buses — 4, 96, 98, 99

Tramways (MET) Omnibus Company (bus fleet operator) — 13, 14, 29, 30, 31, 32, 34, 37, 40 n25, 88, 98, 102

Underground Electric Railways Company — 14

Upton Park (bus garage) — 9

Vanguard (bus fleet operator) — 11

vehicle maintenance during wartime — 56-58, 70

War Department — 90, 92, 98

War Office — 4, 8, 20, 28, 42, 96

War Subvention Scheme — 20, 22, 30, 84

William Beardmore & Company (steelworks) — 78

Wolseley armoured car — 31, 78

Wolseley (vehicle manufacturers) — 11

Wounded soldiers, transported by bus in London — 88

X-type (Daimler) — 84

X-type bus — 12, 15, 88

Y-type lorry, conversion for use as bus — 96, 97, 99, 100 n6

Z-type, see B-type, Russian